BLESSED by the BEST

Understanding the Power, Purpose, and Preservation of God's Blessing

Innocent Chinedu Odinigwe

Copyright @ 2026 Innocent Chinedu Odinigwe

All rights reserved. No part of this publication may be reproduced, stored in a retrieval system, or transmitted in any form or by any means—electronic, mechanical, photocopying, recording, or otherwise—without the prior written permission of the author.

Unauthorized reproduction or distribution of this book, or any portion of it, is strictly prohibited and constitutes a violation of applicable copyright laws. Piracy harms the author's creative rights and is subject to legal action.

All biblical quotations are taken from King James Version (KJV) and New King James Version (NKJV) except where stated otherwise.

ISBN: 979-8-218-89796-3

Edit and Layout by Shonell Bacon
Book Publishing Coach, Telishia Berry

Printed in the United States of America.

PRAISE FOR *BLESSED BY THE BEST*

Adam was not conceived; he was created by God as a full-grown man. There was no nine-month process of development, no gradual formation of organs for functionality. *"And God blessed them"* (Genesis 1:28). The meaning of the word *blessed*, as Apostle Innocent has so eloquently explained, was the bedrock of Adam's sustainability. God endowed him to prosper and succeed on all fronts by using the word *"Be."* It was a direct download from God to man—much like a computer being programmed, with no option but to operate according to its design. However, just as computers can become corrupted by viruses—slowing performance, delaying urgent responses, and detaining, diverting, or defacing positive outcomes—so can man become corrupted by the virus of sin. This corruption permitted the same spirits to attempt interruption of God's eternal plan, purpose, and promises.

In *Blessed by the Best*, Apostle Innocent skillfully and articulately unfolds, through Scripture, the revelation and deep insight of redemption from these diabolical spirits. He shows us the pathway back to God's original intent: to live and thrive in the realm of blessings. When I first heard

Apostle share this revelation, my spirit was instantly emancipated, and I know yours will be as well.

Thank you, Apostle, for sharing this truth, so that generations yet unborn may experience true freedom while walking in the blessings promised by God.

Pastor (Dr) Sarah Morgan
President, Prayer Academy Institute
Los Angeles, California

† † †

Blessed by the Best looks at God's plan for people and the spiritual experiences that shape a believer's life. Using theological ideas, biblical references, and expressive writing, Apostle Innocent Chinedu Odinigwe walks readers through the story of Eden, where God first gave mankind his blessing, purpose, and love. From there, the book tells us that God wants his children to live lives of achievement, authority, and plenty, and that anything short of this is not part of his plan. A key part of this work is its use of Scripture. Each chapter uses the Word, giving both spiritual understanding and doctrinal support.

The author uses descriptive language to show the beauty of creation, God's relationship with man, and the importance of the blessing that directed man's purpose. These scenes give intellectual understanding and emotional depth, calling readers to find the wonder of being created in God's image. The book also stands out by talking about a useful part of Christian life that is often missed: the spiritual forces that keep believers from experiencing God's promises. The author explains five spirits: delay, detention, diversion, deception, and defacement, thereby exposing the enemy's methods and giving readers awareness and good judgment. This makes the book inspirational and helpful, giving tools that speak to the problems that many believers deal with now.

In the end, *Blessed by the Best*'s value comes from its message of hope. It tells readers that God's blessing is not just something from the past, but an active gift meant to support every part of their lives. The tone is positive, asking Christians to be united, stay strong, and believe in a God who restores what was lost. This work is a helpful guide for anyone wanting deeper spiritual understanding, a new sense of purpose, and a better hold on what they have in Christ. It's a well-written addition to Christian writing today that will bless, challenge, and inspire its readers.

Dr. Eugene C. Otuonye
Assistant Principal, Adelanto High School
California, USA
December 2025

DEDICATION

This book is dedicated to my two partners: The Holy Spirit and my wife, Josephine.

Table of Contents

	Foreword	i
	Preface	iii
	Acknowledgments	vii
1	Introduction	1
2	The Spirit of Delay	12
3	Your Blessings Can Be Detained	27
4	The Spirit of Diversion	48
5	The Spirit of Deception	55
6	The Spirit of Defacement	68
7	The Spirit of Divine Blessings	80
	About the Author	97

Foreword

There are books that inform, and there are books that transform. *Blessed by the Best* belongs firmly to the latter. It is a summons to rediscover the original intent of God's blessing upon humanity and to recover the dignity, authority, and purpose that flowed from that divine act.

From its opening lines, the reader is drawn back to Eden—not merely as a place, but as a posture of the soul. With lyrical depth and reverent insight, this work reminds us that the blessing of God preceded human effort or achievement. Before man worked, he was blessed. Before he ruled, he was empowered. Before he acted, capacity was already imparted. This foundational truth, so often overlooked in a performance-driven world, is carefully restored within these pages.

The author skillfully weaves theology, psychology, and spiritual discernment into a single, compelling narrative. He shows that the blessing of God was never intended to inflate ego, fuel materialism, or distract the heart from its Maker. In an age obsessed with gifts but forgetful of the Giver, this book courageously re-centers our attention on presence over possession, communion over consumption.

Perhaps most striking is the book's insistence that God's word both announces and activates destiny. This challenges readers and invites them into a deeper, weightier understanding of stewardship, responsibility, and accountability before God. As the book progresses, it moves into exposing the subtle spiritual adversaries that seek to hinder, delay, distort, or deface the blessings ordained for God's people. With clarity and pastoral concern, the author identifies these forces not to inspire fear, but to awaken discernment and restore confidence in Christ's finished work. The message is clear: what was lost in Adam has been restored in Christ, and no believer is meant to live beneath the inheritance secured for them.

Blessed by the Best is both a mirror and a map. It is a call to maturity, a return to purpose, and a reminder that true blessing is inseparable from obedience, intimacy, and faithfulness. I commend this book to every reader who longs not merely for success, provision, and blessing, but for significance, presence, and the God who blesses. May these pages stir your spirit, steady your faith, and reawaken your confidence that you are, indeed, blessed by the Best.

Pastor (Dr.) James O. Fadel
Continental Overseer, The Redeemed Christian Church of God The Americas 1
515 County Road 1118
Greenville, TX 75401

PREFACE

Doubt has quietly woven its threads into the hearts of many who proclaim the name of Christ-men and women who profess the Christian faith yet remain unsatisfied with their lives. Many cannot reconcile the faith they proclaim with the quality of life they experience. Though our gaze is lifted toward the hills of eternity, Scripture invites us to walk with purpose upon the earth: to be salt that seasons and light that reveals (Matthew 5:13-16; Colossians 3:1-2).

Nowhere in Scripture is a life of quality, fulfillment, or prosperity condemned. On the contrary, the word consistently affirms God's desire to bless the diligent, turn labor into fruit, dreams into reality, and desires into accomplishment (Psalm 1:1-3; Proverbs 10:4). This, too, is why Christ came—to restore all that humanity lost through disobedience in Eden (John 10:10; Luke 19:10).

Nothing in a life filled with pain, perpetual failure, suffering, or disappointment glorifies God. Redemption is holistic—spiritual, physical, and material. As the apostle John prayed, *"Beloved, I wish above all things that thou mayest prosper and be in health, even as thy soul prospereth"* (3 John 1:2). Eden remains God's original blueprint for humanity, a place of unity, love, and abundant provision.

Creation whispers God's love, and redemption amplifies it entirely (Romans 1:20; John 3:16). Within this redemptive program, Paul perceived that in giving us Christ, God also restored every provision necessary for life and godliness (Romans 8:32). These scriptures insist that salvation through Christ reinstates humanity to its pre-fall position. It now rests upon the believer to enter this realm of provision and joy while maintaining a steadfast union with Christ

Yet while redemption is finished and restoration complete, the ancient adversary, who from the beginning usurped man's dominion, has not abandoned his mission (1 Peter 5:8-9). Though defeated, he continues through subtlety and ignorance to persuade many believers that the God who brought Israel out of Egypt cannot sustain them in their wilderness. But nothing is farther from the truth; if He feeds the birds of the air and clothes the lilies of the field, *how much more* will He supply the needs of those He loves? (Matthew 6:26-30; Psalm 145:15-16).

This is the burden and message of this book: to unveil the strategies the enemy employs to make believers fall short of God's promises and blessings. I will expose five specific spirits and their names, operations, and methods while revealing how they contend against believers' God-given inheritance. This truth transcends denominations and doctrines, uniting the entire body of Christ against a common enemy. It is time we focus more on what unites us than on what divides us (Ephesians 4:1-6).

As you patiently turn these pages, you will discover that the stories recorded in Scripture mirror the realities of our contemporary struggles. *"For whatsoever things were written aforetime were written for our learning, that we through patience and comfort of the Scriptures might have hope"* (Romans 15:4). In your hand is a tool for restoration, an answer to unspoken frustrations, and a guide through the troubling puzzles of life. Different chapters will discuss the ministry of these spirits and their strategies: delay, detain, divert, deceive, and deface.

ACKNOWLEDGMENTS

I'd like to say thank you, God, whose grace made this work possible. Boniface and Agnes Odinigwe (of blessed memory), for their love and nurturing. Theresa Mogor (of blessed memory), the mother of my wife, for her enduring legacy.

Mother Delores Chatman for her care; Ty-lesha Jones, whose sponsorship supported this publication; Jude and Linda Njoku, my trusted confidants; Christiana Ibeabuchi, an encourager; Sharon Doyle, who did the typing; Shamel Payne, my armor bearer; Anna Brown, for caring for my mother; Angel Iyoha Agbaosi, for timely words of encouragement; Clement and Felicia Ajayi, for their gifts and support. Miriam Odinigwe, your hours spent on this project fueled my determination.

To all who prayed, encouraged, and stood with me—Janet Baratta, Yinka Orekoya, Kathy Jones, Andrew and Tutu Adesida, Ronika Jones, Shanika Payne, Yinka and Ogonna Adeola-Hazzan, Tricia Vargas, Karen Robertson, Uloma Anozie, Ray and Char Hogan, Joseph and Yemi Oyeyemi, Ogueri Nwosu, Orenda Waters, Chioma Moughalu, Ngozi Anyanacho, Jesse Morgan, April Washington, Ijeoma Otuechere, Joyce Jackson, Monica Gill—Thank you.

I

INTRODUCTION

The lofty trees, as far as his eyes could wander, with their rich foliage of living green carefully planted by the riverside, stood as a testament and handiwork of an esteemed Gardener.

The Garden of Man

The early morning dew did fall upon his untainted soul, mingling with those soothing words that greeted his ears. Straightway, the feeling of unfamiliarity and strangeness vanished from his heart. Sweet and pleasant words from the lips of his Creator cemented a bond of eternal purpose with earthly gratification. Adam's eyes opened to behold the beauty of the flowers of the garden, glowing from a bare earth and circled round with lonely hills. The melody rising from the scintillating songs of the birds, making the very air vocal with their happy songs, pulled a chord of crescendo within his heart. The lofty trees, as far as his eyes could wander, with their rich foliage of living green carefully planted by the riverside, stood as a testament and handiwork of an esteemed Gardener. Yet above all that might be seen, touched, or heard, nothing came near the presence of his Maker, which captivated both his spirit and soul with the very definition of purpose and a firm assurance that he was no spiritual accident. With beauty round about the place where God set him (Genesis 2:8), and a journey ordained from the womb of eternity, man stood at the threshold of his beginning. The breath of the Almighty still warm upon his frame, he beheld creation in its morning glory. And even as his heart musing upon his mission and the solemn charge that awaited him, the Most High inclined His voice toward the *dust-formed king*.

Then God spoke the first word into his ears-the first words ever to grace human ears, and words heavy with promise, pregnant with destiny and resounding with eternal weight: *"Be fruitful, and multiply, and replenish the earth, and subdue it: and have dominion..."* (Genesis 1:28). Behold the richness of that divine utterance: the promise of fruitfulness, the power of multiplication, the sacred duty of replenishment, the authority to subdue rebellion, and the sovereignty of dominion—all descending like dew from the lips of God.

Yet all these heavenly mandates flowed from a single, thunderous proclamation: "And God blessed them." From that blessing sprang mission. From that blessing came identity. From that blessing rose the dignity of dominion. But here is a question we must pause and ponder: **was this blessing only but a word spoken, or was it an act wrought by the hand of God?** In my humble submission with reverent persuasion, I hold that the blessing was an action performed even before the word was spoken, for in the realm of the spirit, the deed and the declaration are intertwined; His speech does not merely describe.

It accomplishes. His word does not linger powerless; it performs.

Therefore, when "God blessed them," He did not merely announce possibility; He activated destiny. He did not merely speak potential; He imparted power. He did not merely command; He conferred capacity. The blessing was not a wish. It was an endowment with power for the journey ahead. And so, before man ever tilled the soil, fruitfulness was already deposited in him. Before ever he lifted his eyes to the horizon, multiplication was already alive within him. Before ever his feet touched the dust of the earth, dominion had already crowned him. Such is the nature of God's blessing—it does not wait for your effort to begin its work. It acts before you act. It empowers before you attempt. It goes before you as promise and follows behind you as fulfillment (Psalm 23:6).

The Psychology of the Blessing

Yet the blessing pronounced upon man was given with due diligence to collaborate with the Creator's divine ideology and eternal purpose.

Both Creator and creation were encapsulated in a perfect union and harmony that reflected divine will, delight, and purpose. The work of creation was completed, and God entered into His rest. The sacred council of heaven had crowned creation, perfecting the project by making man after the similitude of God, that he might exercise oversight upon the whole earth. His influence could not be defined by scope, for even the vastness of the ocean alone is beyond the ability of the most cunning genius to measure. The sky, bright with innumerable stars, lies beyond his cognitive reach to number. The animals of various species, both great and small, will be too swift to pursue, too mighty to subdue, too perilous to tame, and too little to reckon with. Yet the blessing pronounced upon man was given with due diligence to collaborate with the Creator's divine ideology and eternal purpose. This pronouncement of blessing upon Adam and Eve was not that man's mind should be puffed up with wealth under his command, nor that he parade himself with the charade of materialism to display affluence and flamboyance, but that his heart might never depart from the eternal purpose for which God planted him in a garden where he had no cause to want—The Psalmist declared, "The Lord is my Shepherd, I shall not want..." (Psalm 23:1).

The blessing placed upon man, along with the earthly riches and provisions entrusted to him, was designed to harmonize his soul with the peace that flows only from God, peace reserved for those whose minds remain steadfast upon Him (Isaiah 26:3). For from the beginning, the Creator shaped a world both beautiful and bountiful, and into this sacred harmony, He breathed His blessing, that humanity might walk in communion with His divine rest. This blessing was not merely adornment, nor a gift meant to dazzle the senses, but a spiritual alignment -an internal melody binding man to the heart of his Maker.

It was the benediction that crowned creation: "And God blessed them..." (Genesis 1:28). A blessing meant to anchor man in divine serenity, to steady his steps, to enrich his purpose, and to remind him that true abundance springs not from the earth, but from the God who formed it.

The Gift and the Giver

The pressure and pursuit after the gift without the Giver lead only to perversion, abuse, and the making of a quasi-god—under which mankind becomes slave to that which purpose ordained him ruler.

The gift and the Giver are inextricably knit together and must be received with contentment and gratitude, with the Giver esteemed far more honorable than the gift. The pressure and pursuit after the gift without the Giver lead only to perversion, abuse, and the making of a quasi-god, under which mankind becomes slave to that which purpose ordained him ruler. This is the iconic "garden" from which God bequeathed all His creation to man through dominion mandate and willed the entire earth with all its resources to him through love, purpose, and affection. This is the first establishment of trust given to man, a responsibility that he must account for, and the territory where everything else is subordinate to him. Have you paused to think about the psychology of the blessing bestowed upon you and I? That everything else derive their fulfillment and purpose through their loyalty to man? This could be difficult to concede, but the reality is not too far-fetched, for even the furniture within your household were once standing as lonely trees in the forest, or raw materials hidden beneath the earth until man sought them out. It is beyond my imagination that the entire earth which God holds total ownership was graciously given over to man.

Listen again to the Psalmist: *"The earth is the Lord's, and the fullness thereof, the world and all who dwell therein"* (Psalm 24:1). *"The heaven, Even the heavens, are the Lord's: but the earth hath he given to the children of men"* (Psalm 115:16).

There is no length that love cannot go, no depth it cannot reach in expressing itself. This is profoundly true of God—in creation, in provision, in redemption, and in restoration. The voice of the Lord came walking in the garden of Eden—that gentle, sacred visitation (Genesis 3:8). This daily communion reveals a craving in the heart of God, prompted by a desire for intimacy, driven by a longing whose satisfaction was tailored to one particular being—man. It is this singular act, among many, that amplifies the sacred bond between the gift and the Giver. For in walking toward man, God unveiled a love that seeks fellowship, a love that does not remain distant, a love that bends low to share the coolness of the day with the one He formed (Genesis 2:7). Here, the blessing proved again to rise far above material possession, for what is provision compared to Presence? What is abundance beside communion? In Eden, God showed that the highest blessing is not the garden's beauty nor its riches, but the God who walks within it. *But love can grant only what faithfulness can retain, Selah.*

The Theology of the Blessing

Had man not been the crown of creation for coordination, the beauty of the entire earth would have faded, and creation swallowed in chaos.

The idea to make man was followed thus: "So God created man in His own image; in the image of God created He him; male and female created He them." Mark the language of Scripture— "created He him." A creative force, far more than a constructive work, is revealed in this making of man. Consider this awhile: the whole earth holds room enough to house every product of the Creator.

The airspace, free and unperturbed, grants liberty to birds to flap their wings as they migrate from coast to coast. The ocean, vast and varied, is a home both to the mighty whale and the dwarf minnow—the genius paedocypris wiggling in murky waters of the peat swamps of Southeast Asia. The world of oceans, seas, rivers, and streams, claiming seventy percent of the earth's expanse, is an unbroken testament leaving no room for scientific denial that the intelligence behind the ecosystem is wholly outsourced. Think also of the land, a habitat for both great and small. The beasts of many kinds and sizes are dwellers therein, crafting for themselves safe havens for survival and posterity. Had man not been the crown of creation for coordination, the beauty of the entire earth would have faded, and creation swallowed in chaos. Man stepped upon the stage with a dual necessity: to point creation toward God for His pleasure and to give creation purpose and fulfillment. Therefore, "God blessed them."

Man, placed at the very center of creation, stands as a strong ally and partner in God's eternal agenda, a co-laborer in shaping the earth into a colony of heaven (Matthew 6:10). The blessings of God bestowed upon him carry within them a depth of divine theology, truths that must never slip from our minds, lest purpose be swallowed by vain pursuits and hollow ambitions. These blessings must rise within us like a holy imagination, commanding our daily meditation, that man, the *earthly governor* crowned with glory and honor (Psalm 8:5-6), has been entrusted with the sacred responsibility of coordinating all that his Maker placed in the realm of earth to harmonize with the government of heaven.

This truth is deeper than the thrill of endless discoveries; it is a summons to sober reflection, awakening the heart to its Source, and grounding the soul in the weight of stewardship. For only with such understanding can man carry out his duty—not only with responsibility, but with gladness, humility, and the steady hope of the eternal reward promised to the faithful: "Well done, thou good and faithful servant" (Matthew 25:21).

That moment of crowning remains sacred, a moment when faithfulness rises to defend the trust love once placed in us, and the blessings we carried become clearer than ever: they were never trophies of possession, but purpose-driven vessels, divine provisions meant to support the journey, fuel the stewardship, and anchor the heart to the One who gave them. This is the theology of the blessing.

And God Blessed Them

This blessing was far more than provision for earthly needs or luxuries.

Again, all that God does is purposeful. Every creation must rely upon His sovereign will and pleasure—*"Thou art worthy to receive glory and honor and power, for thou hast created all things, and for thy pleasure they are and were created"* (Revelations 4:11). Thus, nothing outside His purpose holds legitimacy of existence nor bears the guarantee of sustaining His divine intent. When God blessed man, He set him upon a path to coordinate collective fulfillment and adherence to His sacred goals in all creation. Only man can discern the fingerprint of God upon all He has touched or made. Knowing well that the earth would one day come under luciferous vices—a rebellion born first in heaven—God, out of necessity, crowned His creation with blessing: "And God blessed them."

This blessing was far more than provision for earthly needs or luxuries. Make no mistake: these crowning words of God expressed both love and purpose. Love, in that man, so dear to His heart, is the expression of His invisible nature and attributes. Purpose, in that man must function above all else He made, with intelligence for coordination, management, and supervision. A creature so superior as man is, among many things, a tapestry woven with countless moments, emotions, memories, and experiences. It is this understanding, deeper than the thought expressed so far can compose such a poetry:

Be fruitful,

And multiply,

And replenish,

And subdue it,

And have dominion over the fish of the sea,

And over the fowl of the air,

And over every living thing that moveth upon the earth... (Genesis 1:28).

Each pronouncement echoes deep into the heart of man beyond the mere sound of words. God's love bestowed a task mingled with affection. Man's mandate is crowned with power to ensure that heaven and earth remain in harmony under his governance. Verily, the blessing is the machinery necessary to fulfill his purpose. Therefore, every created thing must surrender its virtue beneath the authority of man—the chosen agent to coordinate their movements and align them with divine counsel. To perform such a task and stand in the spotlight, his garment must remain unsoiled and his head anointed continually: *"Let thy garment be always white, and let thy head lack no ointment"* (Ecclesiastes 9:8). Only through such a state can man retain the nature that elevates him above all creation. Thus, the blessing is proven again to be far more than earthly possession.

Mark well how God fashioned His speech to impress the rhythm of His heart upon the man. Each line was joined with "And," expressing a continuation of impartation and the sealing of a bond with love. The garden's atmosphere received each word with bliss, infusing into every plant and creature—animate and inanimate, visible and invisible—the power to fulfill their purposes through loyalty to man. God's blessing upon beings such as you and I is a seal of approval, an expression of love, and the force behind success and victory. Nothing comes your way that the blessing may not challenge and bend to purpose! Truly, you are blessed by the Best.

A question now arises: Are we enjoying the blessings of the Lord? Are we seeing the manifestations of His promises, or witnessing otherwise in our lives? This inquiry shall shape our further discourse in the chapters ahead. It is my humble submission that many fall short of God's promises and manifestations. Though our struggles vary, the pain, suffering, disappointments, and failures bring kindred frustration to many souls. Thus, the goal of this book is to discover the factors responsible for the present state of many of God's children.

No doubt many are living out their dreams, rejoicing in the goodness of God, and fulfilling their visions. So, it ought to be, and we are grateful on their behalf. Yet because we journey together, and because our mission is to leave no one behind, an offense against one is an offense against all. Thus, Christ likened the Church to the human body—the body of Christ, of which we are components. Though differing in role, we are united in one purpose. It is imperative that the body rise against a common enemy—a pandemic bedeviling us, spreading across the globe, and dampening our faith in the God who is able to do all according to His will. Our service must be rendered with gladness, our faith untainted, and our fellowship unmixed with strife.

Join me, therefore, as we expose the subtle tricks of the enemy and how he manipulates believers out of their God-given blessings, causing them to live a substituted life with little to show that their Savior restored all that was lost through Adam's disobedience. Blessings descend from the spiritual realm for earthly manifestation. Should the enemy wish to hinder them, he must enlist spiritual agents to do so. What we behold in the natural is but a reflection of the spiritual state. I will be exposing five spirits through which the enemy interferes with your blessings, and how these spirits operate. This work will be both revelatory and riveting as we discuss how Satan can do the either of the following to your God-given blessings:

- † Delay (spirit of delay)
- † Detain (spirit of detention)
- † Divert (spirit of diversion)
- † Deceive (spirit of deception)
- † Deface (spirit of defacement)

Thus begins the enemy's first strike, the subtle snare of the spirit of delay against our promised blessings.

2

THE SPIRIT OF DELAY

From the time of man's conception to the time of his transition, time has always been the umpire of his success or failure.

Many believers today are behind schedule in many ways. Time cannot be separated from man in all his activities and life. Time regulates most of our activities and helps to keep us on track. From the time of man's conception to the time of his transition, time has always been the umpire of his success or failure: *"A time to be born and a time to die; a time to plant and a time to pluck up that which is planted"* (Ecclesiastes 3:2). Clearly, this scripture points to the role that time plays in every aspect of life and nature as it pertains to the purpose of man on earth. Subsequently, everything is supposed to follow the rhythm of time and season. To believe otherwise is to imagine that purpose was never woven into God's hands as He shaped you in your mother's womb (Jeremiah 1:5). Such a thought does not merely wander, it wounds, striking at the very heart of destiny and dimming the brilliance of God's design. It would leave us drifting like leaves on the winds of chance, prisoners of luck and randomness. And what is a plan without time? What is a strategy without seasons? The ordained pathway by which purpose comes to bloom. Time, therefore, is not an afterthought. It is the sacred rhythm through which destiny unfolds, the ordained pathway by which purpose comes to bloom.

But if, like me, you believe in purpose, then it follows that every divine program carries both timing and strategy. For the Lord Himself declares, "I know the plans I have for you... plans for good and not for evil" (Jeremiah 29:11). And plans, by their very nature, unfold within appointed times.

It is safe to say that there is a time to ask from God and a time to receive that which He has promised— "Ask, and you shall receive..." (Matthew 7:7). Ideally, we can conclude that everything ought to happen at the proper time. A woman carries a baby for nine months before delivery, which allows proper development of the child. But what happens when the baby shows no sign of development and readiness for delivery? This could cause a medical problem, because no matter how much a baby grows in the mother's womb, adulthood cannot be achieved within the walls of the uterus—this is a case of delay.

Also, when a couple enters into a union of matrimony, all eyes turn to them, and parents await good news after some period of their union. The couple may plan their family and future by deliberately waiting, which is understandable, but if that is not the case, delay could be in effect through barrenness. Raising children at an old age has its own liabilities, deprivation, and imbalance within the family system. The same can be said about a woman who has advanced in age before getting married to start a family.

What about a young man who works very hard, either as a private business owner or one who spends years in the public sector but has nothing to show for it? Such a man may not be on a timely schedule to achieve his goals, dreams, and aspirations in life as they relate to time. The tragedy of delay is that most people do not live to enjoy the fruit of their labor.

It is my prayer over you, my esteemed reader, that you shall not build a home for another to inhabit, neither shall you plant for another to eat. *"They shall not build, and another inhabit; they shall not plant, and another eat: for as the days of a tree are the days of my people, and My elect shall long enjoy the work of their hands"* (Isaiah 65:22).

Walk With God

God is never late!

God is never late! He has time in His hands. The palpitation of the heart is a prime assurance that when God becomes the regulator of your activities by walking closely with Him, you shall not skip a beat. The Scriptures assure us that God makes all things beautiful in His own time. He makes all things attractive, delightful, and pleasing in His own time. Time is absolutely important both for God and for man.

Every path that leads to success, victory, and dream fulfillment is familiar to men and women who walk with God and never miss a step. Learn to be on God's schedule through faith, obedience, and total dependence on Him, and all things shall become beautiful in your life.

Be Sober and Vigilant—Spiritual Surveillance.

We must confront ignorance with audacity and welcome knowledge with tenacity.

The spirit of delay is a quiet snare, one of the enemy's subtle arts for wearying the believer's soul. To escape its grip, we must awaken our spiritual senses, discerning whether we are truly waiting on God or slowly surrendering our years to futility. Apostle Peter urges us to be "sober and vigilant" (1 Peter 5:8), for the adversary prowls tirelessly, releasing his schemes and agents to dim the vibrant life Christ promised, a life meant to be abundant, present, and overflowing (John 10:10).

If there is anything the devil desires, it is to turn the camera around and make God appear to be a liar, unfaithful and inadequate to keep His promises. No mortal would want to pledge allegiance to a God who cannot deliver and accomplish His promises. When the integrity of any deity to be faithful to promises and able in performance becomes questionable, such a deity—though radiant as the sun in appearance, sophisticated in composition, and pristine in glory—yet still revered by those who pledge allegiance, no longer holds a place of true loyalty and love unrestrained. Religion takes the place of relationship, ritualism overshadows reverence, and doubt evicts faith from every chamber of the heart. This is the negative that the devil develops in the darkest room of ignorance, parading themselves in various religious organizations and movements which only move followers away from the "Truth," who is the true and living God. But we know that our God is faithful to His promises, able to perform according to His words. This is why our service to Him is done with gladness and utmost gratification. In order to achieve such a state of spiritual ecstasy, we must confront ignorance with audacity and welcome knowledge with tenacity. This book is mission-driven to accomplish so. Keep reading!

Devil's Option

What the devil cannot deny, he attempts to delay.

The devil knows that God is faithful. He knows that God is able, loving, caring, and unchanging. He also knows from the creation of man that the Creator sealed him with blessing. Every time a man enters into the closet to pray, he draws from a fountain that never runs dry. Our God is the undeniable source of all resources.

This is an assurance that our prayers, carried out with faith, are guaranteed to be answered with tangible results. No doubt the enemy is threatened when we rise to a level of knowledge and awareness that exposes "the wiles of the devil." Imagine how great our victory would be when, like our Maker, we understand that "neither is there any creature that is not manifest in His sight, but all things are naked and opened unto the eyes of Him with whom we have to do" (Hebrews 4:13).

Nothing hidden cannot be revealed. Our responsibility is to search diligently and trust in the guidance of the Holy Spirit to open our understanding into hidden things through knowledge and revelation. This is where the journey of success begins, and a life of breakthroughs and prosperity becomes inevitable.

The goal of restoration is to bring man back to the place of his original state, where he was crowned with blessing from God. The Holy Spirit is committed to bringing us back to Eden and endowing us with power and authority. You are in a season that requires absolute soberness, attentiveness to prophecy, and proper spiritual accountability.

Delay: The Oxford Dictionary defines delay as "to make someone or something late or slow." Could it be that the spirit of delay has been deployed against your blessing? Could this explain why you work like an elephant but eat like an ant? Could this be the reason for your frustrations and discouragement because what you have been waiting for has not yet arrived?

The spirit of delay has one assignment, to slow the arrival or manifestation of the promises of God in your life. The devil knows he cannot stop God from answering your prayers because you sealed them with faith and thanksgiving, and he is aware that God answers when the righteous call upon His name. What the devil cannot deny, he attempts to delay.

Instances of How the Spirit of Delay Came In

Although we may not always arrive at the same time, the important thing is not to show up when the market is over.

Everything ought to happen at its proper time. Life is staged to be so. Although we may not always arrive at the same time, the important thing is not to show up when the market is over. Returning to Genesis 11, something important is revealed in the family history of Abraham, rooted from Arphaxad to Nahor, Abraham's grandfather. A common pattern is clear—the men in this family achieved certain milestones within a specific age bracket. From ages 29 to 35, from Arphaxad to Nahor, these men were marrying and having children. That pattern continued until the name Terah was mentioned. Terah was the father of Abraham. Notice something unusual: Terah fell out of the pattern and was 70 years old when he began to have children—Abraham, Nahor, and Haran. The shift is too radical to ignore.

Why 70 years when others achieved similar milestones at ages 29 to 35? The answer is not far-fetched—the spirit of delay had entered to alter the pattern within the lineage. Does this sound familiar to you? Could this be what you are dealing with? Are names and situations flashing in your mind right now? Perhaps you are shaking your head or drowning in thought. This is exactly what this book intends to accomplish in every reader, because you are about to unravel a puzzle many before you never dared to confront.

Terah's delay was not accidental; it was a spiritual intrusion meant to distort a God-ordained pattern. Though he eventually fathered children, delay had already dug its claws into his destiny. Delay is subtle, it creeps in quietly like a shadow stretching itself across generations. If not confronted, it becomes a family inheritance, passed from father to son and mother to daughter.

Patterns do not lie. They speak loudly to the discerning. What repeats itself in silence may be shouting in the spirit realm. Many people today live within cycles they did not create—cycles planted long before their birth, strengthened by ignorance and maintained by inaction. But when knowledge comes, the cycle must bow.

Abraham inherited not only the blessings but also the battle against delay. Though God called him blessed, the fulfillment of the promise seemed to tarry. Yet delay is not denial. When God speaks, His word stands. God separated Abraham from his father's house—a divine intervention against inherited delay. Sometimes God must strip you of familiar surroundings to clothe you with a new destiny.

Delay affects childbirth, marriage, career, finances, ministry, and spiritual growth. Many find themselves stuck at the same point year after year. That is the nature of delay—it builds invisible barriers only revelation and spiritual warfare can uproot.

Delay steals seasons. A stolen season means a stolen opportunity. Yet what the enemy delays, God restores with interest. God dwells outside time yet governs time. He compresses years into moments and moments into miracles. Your journey to freedom begins with awareness. Once you discern the pattern, confront it. Heaven backs the bold: "The kingdom of heaven suffereth violence, and the violent take it by force." You are stepping into revelation, and revelation is the birthplace of deliverance.

The Place of Warfare

Saints of God, awake for here lies the cause why spiritual warfare prayer is most needful for the securing of victory. Michael the Archangel, valiant in the arts of war, beareth the sword of conflict; and the scriptures declare, "the kingdom of God suffereth violence, and the violent take it by force."

When shall you rise up in holy indignation to confront the enemies that stand against your breakthrough? The hour is now! Break every demonic vault! Break every engagement, every encasement, every entanglement, and every trap of darkness. Loose the chains that bind you in the name of Jesus. I stand in concord with you that every spirit claiming a hold, an influence, or an authority over your life shall be consumed by holy fire in the name of Jesus. Every affiliation, every association, every covenant or inherited tie, through bloodline, marriage, or the bearing of a name, whereby the enemy delays your blessing, is broken this day in Jesus' mighty name.

Overcoming the Spirit of Delay

The spirit of delay is a cruel adversary. It stretches time, burdens the heart, and frustrates the dreams that God has planted within His people. Yet, Scripture reveals that God has never left His children without remedies for this spiritual affliction. There are many measures one can take to alleviate the pain caused by delay and to enjoy the riches of serving God. But for the sake of time and space, I will highlight two essential and transformative measures: Divine Speed.

Throughout the Bible, we find men and women who battled delays—some for years, others for decades. Yet these same individuals eventually encountered supernatural interventions that broke the hold of delay and ushered them into accelerated fulfillment. Their stories remind us that *we too shall overcome,* and their testimonies will one day be ours.

In The Case of Jehu—Rediscovered Destiny 1 Kings 19:15-17, God instructed the prophet Elijah to anoint three men:

† Elisha to succeed him as prophet,
† Hazael to become king over Syria,
† Jehu to become king of Israel.

Elijah found Elisha and subsequently anointed him after he proved his commitment through service. Hazael also rose to kingship according to the prophetic word (2 Kings 8:13). But Jehu—Jehu seemed to vanish.

His prolonged absence caused many hearts to question the prophetic accuracy of God's word over his life. Although Scripture does not reveal how many years passed, the spirit of delay clearly worked against him. Yet God's word does not fail (Isaiah 55:11). At the appointed time, Jehu resurfaced, and Elisha's servant found him and anointed him king in the place of Ahab (2 Kings 9:1-3).

Notice the express instruction of Elisha to the servant on an urgent errand: *"When you arrive, look for Jehu..."* He had to be found. To *find* a thing suggests it was misplaced. To *find* someone implies a search. Jehu had drifted into obscurity, his destiny seemingly buried under the weight of delay. But God sent a servant to search him out, a divine reminder that heaven never loses sight of what delay attempts to hide.

The manner of Jehu's anointing is profoundly revealing. Elisha commanded the young prophet to act with urgency:

† Find Jehu
† Take him to an inner chamber
† Anoint him quickly
† Then open the door and run

This urgency signified the breaking of delay. In God's kingdom, divine speed is the antidote to spiritual stagnation. When a life has wandered, wavered, or wallowed in indecision, divine speed redeems lost time (Ephesians 5:16).

The Anointing of Divine Speed

Divine speed collapses the long processes that time demands. What takes others ten years can happen for you in ten months. A project that takes five years can be accomplished in five months. When God steps into a man's timeline, the "horror of time" and the anxiety of delay lose their power.

When divine speed rests upon an individual, the results are astonishing, mind-boggling accomplishments within impossible timeframes. Their movements change.

Their outlook shifts. They become allergic to procrastination and hostile to a "tomorrow attitude." They speak of the urgency of now, driven by passion and clothed with zeal (Romans 12:11).

This was Jehu.

Long before anyone recognized his face, people recognized his movement. In 2 Kings 9:20, the watchman exclaimed, *"The driving is like the driving of Jehu... for he driveth furiously."* That was the character of a man operating under divine acceleration. Delay had wasted years, but speed recovered them.

Your Season of Acceleration

This is what you need in this season: uncommon speed and supernatural acceleration to catch up and overtake the years stolen by delay. God promises that you will move swiftly, recover fully, and arrive exactly where you should have been—by His hand, not by your effort. There is hope for you in God. Your story is about to turn suddenly. *"For the vision is yet for an appointed time... though it tarry, wait for it; it will surely come, it will not delay"* (Habakkuk 2:3).

Elijah: Running Beyond Time

Another example is the prophet Elijah. After three and a half years of drought, God was ready to send rain (1 Kings 18:41–46). Elijah bowed before God in prayer to birth the new season. He heard the sound of rain in the spirit, though nothing in the natural suggested anything was coming.

This mirrors our own lives: when situations last too long, they become part of us. Many settled for less and mistake satanic substitutes for God's will. Yet God desires to change that mindset, to teach us that prolonged struggle is not permanent.

Elijah told Ahab to mount his chariot and run, for he heard the sound of abundance. What you hear in the spirit determines how you respond in life. Some hear fear, discouragement, and defeat. But for you, this message is the sound of accomplishment, the assurance that *delay is not denial.*

The drought ended, but it ended with an anointing of speed. Ahab rode ahead on a chariot, but *"the hand of the Lord came upon Elijah,"* and the old prophet outran the king to Jezreel. Divine speed makes the impossible ordinary. Age does not disqualify you. Past failure does not disqualify you. Delay does not disqualify you. Elijah was old, yet he ran with the strength of the Spirit. *"The race is not to the swift, nor the battle to the strong"* (Ecclesiastes 9:11).

You can still outrun your enemies. You can still arrive on time. You can still fulfill your God-given destiny. Elijah reached the gates of Jezreel ahead of Ahab, a proof that supernatural acceleration redeems wasted years.

Restoration of Years

Another powerful way to overcome the spirit of delay is through *divine restoration.* In 1 Samuel 30, the Amalekites invaded Ziklag and carried away David's wives, children, and the families of the men who had gone to battle with him. They had been gone for seventy-two hours, and in any battle, whether spiritual or natural, seventy-two hours can change everything.

David, overwhelmed with grief yet refusing to surrender to despair, turned to the Lord and inquired whether he should pursue the Amalekites and if there was still a possibility of catching up with them. His prayer reveals an important truth: time had already passed, and it was no longer in his favor. By every natural standard, recovery was impossible. But the voice of God intervened.

The Lord answered David saying, *"Pursue, for you shall surely overtake them, and without fail recover all"* (1 Samuel 30:8). God overturned the disadvantage of time and empowered David with supernatural speed, strategy, and strength. This same word is echoing to you today. It is never too late to recover the years and everything the enemy has taken from you.

David needed more than permission to pursue; he needed assurance that:

† he could overtake, and
† he would without fail recover all.

The phrase *"without fail"* is the seal of divine guarantee, an assurance only God can give through supernatural intervention. My esteemed reader, this is the same assurance God gives you today: you shall pursue, you shall overtake, and you shall, without **fail**, recover ALL!

God confirms this promise again in Joel 2:25, saying: *"I will restore to you the years that the locust, the cankerworm, the caterpillar, and the palmerworm have eaten."*

This is not merely the restoration of things. It is *the restoration of years*:

† years of waste,
† years of fruitlessness,
† years of frustration,
† years of failure, and
† years of disappointment.

The God who restores time is promising to return to you everything the spirit of delay has eaten: your ministry, your business, your finances, your marriage, your children, your health, your opportunities, and everything that concerns your destiny in the mighty name of Jesus.

3

YOUR BLESSINGS CAN BE DETAINED

When the enemy sees that his foothold of delay has gone unchallenged, he advances to his next strategy—detention.

One of the realities we have come to understand about the enemy is that he is exceedingly crafty—subtle, silent, and often undetected. He exercises a sly ability to slip into a person's life, a family, a ministry, a marriage, or any sphere where he is carelessly granted a foothold. Apostle Paul warns us in Ephesians 4:27, *"Neither give place to the devil."* This image of a *foothold* is not mere metaphor—it is a spiritual law: whatever space the enemy is allowed, he will attempt to expand.

In the previous chapter, we examined the spirit of delay. When the enemy introduces delay into your prayers, breakthroughs, promotions, fruitfulness, dreams, visions, elevation, and all areas of your life, he also studies your response. Our charge is to resist him with everything we possess—through fervent prayer (James 5:16), faith-filled confession (Mark 11:23-24), and the authority given to us in Christ (Luke 10:19).

Your response becomes a declaration to the spirit of delay that you will not exchange joy for sorrow. Many believers have known the moment when they must speak into the atmosphere with holy authority—just as David spoke to Goliath (1 Samuel 17:45), or as Jesus rebuked the storm (Mark 4:39), refusing to allow darkness to dictate the narrative.

Beloved, you must learn to be spiritually assertive. A radical anointing for radical believers is needed in our time. When the enemy sees that his foothold of delay has gone unchallenged, he advances to his next strategy—detention.

Power Codes in the Spirit

In the realm of the spirit, my brethren, lie depths unfathomable, layouts unseen, dimensions innumerable, and power codes through which victory is received.

There is a great and urgent need for knowledge within the Body of Christ—yes, knowledge that reach beyond the first confession that Jesus Christ died on the cross for our sins. Though this confession be the sure foundation of our faith, it is not the pinnacle. No—it is but the beginning, upon which spiritual advancement must be built.

In the realm of the spirit, my brethren, lie depths unfathomable, layouts unseen, dimensions innumerable, and power codes through which victory is received. Intellectual engagement with the mysteries of God has long been the secret behind the mighty exploits wrought by God's generals. No believer may function beyond the horizon of their understanding. Neither can you manifest beyond the measure of your knowledge and encounters. For not everything within the spirit realm may be imitated; authorization and identity are forged through divine encounters alone. How painful to know that many believers wander in cycles instead of moving forward. True spirituality is ever-progressive, whereas routine religious practices often yield but meager fruit.

Names, dear brethren, bear power. They serve as emblems of identity and seals of divine intention. Since spirits respond to names, the Almighty give names with precision and purpose. Hidden truths lie within the name changes in the scripture—Abram to Abraham, Sarai to Sarah, Simon to Peter, Saul to Paul, Jacob to Israel. This is the mystery of names—one of the ancient power codes of the spirit.

The Mystery and Power of Names

Some names summon divine aid; others stir negative reactions among spirits.

Spirits discern names. A name may bear weight in the spirit, or it may be as naught. Therefore, the first threshold of engagement in spiritual warfare is the securing of identity. "Who are you?" remains the question echoed in the spirit realm—just as it was asked of the seven sons of Sceva: "Jesus I know, and Paul I know, but who are you?"

Authority lies hidden in identity. Some names summon divine aid; others stir negative reactions among spirits. God has bestowed upon Jesus a name above all other names, that at the very mention thereof, every knee should bow—whether in heaven, on earth, or beneath the earth. Think upon the power in that name alone: healing, deliverance, salvation. Even so, your own name carries spiritual consequence. It is incumbent on you dear esteemed reader to find out the meaning behind your name.

When Daniel set forth upon his twenty-one-day fast, he dwelt within the region of Babylon—a territory rife with demonic strongholds. His very identity had been pressed upon by the Babylonian name they gave him. For this cause, territorial powers rose up to challenge the right of God's angel to traverse their domain. The angel was detained until Michael came forth with superior authority.

Hear now this prophecy: In the name of Jesus—the name exalted above all—every blessing that pertains to you, yet has been detained by reason of portals, names, bloodlines, or unholy contact, is loosed this very day. No more detention, in Jesus' name.

Much transpires within the unseen realm, such as casualties, diversions, delays, and frustrations. Many blessings, marriages, financial provisions, and opportunities remain under demonic arrest. And believers, wearied by delay, begin to ponder if the Lord has forsaken them. But you must rise and seize that which heaven has already released to you.

Elijah understood the tracking in the spirit. With his face bowed between his knees, he sent forth his servant time and again to behold the horizon until evidence appeared (1 Kings 18:42–43). For prayer without watching is but spiritual slumber. Didn't Christ command us to watch and pray? Therefore, awaken your senses, that you may discern your blessings are being challenged. I will suggest that if your present strategy in prayer is ineffective and unable to deliver the result you are looking for, then you must shift your posture. A new strategy will always produce a new result.

The Weight of Detention

To *detain* means to restrain, hold back, or keep from moving forward. Many of God's blessings intended for His people have been held in *illegal spiritual custody*, often because the believer remains unaware or passive. Scripture provides several profound examples of this reality:

1. *Daniel's Blessing Detained in the Heavens* (Daniel 10:12-13). Daniel prayed, and God answered immediately—"from the first day." Yet the answer was detained for twenty-one days by the prince of Persia, a demonic principality. A spiritual embargo was placed on Daniel's blessing until Michael the archangel intervened. This is a vivid biblical example of blessings being detained, not denied.

2. *Paul's Hindrance by Satan* (1 Thessalonians 2:18). Paul desired to visit the Thessalonian church, but he wrote, *"We would have come unto you... but Satan hindered us."* The Greek term implies blocking a road, placing spiritual obstructions— detainment.

3. *Israel's Delayed Promise in the Wilderness* (Numbers 14:34). God promised them a land flowing with milk and honey, yet unbelief and spiritual carelessness detained the manifestation of that promise for forty years. The blessing existed.

The promise was sure. But the people's posture allowed the enemy to take advantage.

4. *The Apostle Peter Targeted for Detainment* (Acts 12:4–5). Herod arrested Peter and placed him under heavy guard to detain the movement of the Gospel. But the church prayed "without ceasing" (v. 5), and God sent an angel to break the detainment. Prayer shattered the spiritual embargo.

5. *Jesus' Parable of the Strong Man* (Mark 3:27). Jesus reveals that blessings held in captivity require spiritual force: *"No man can enter a strong man's house and spoil his goods, except he first bind the strong man."* The "goods" represent blessings detained in enemy custody. The "binding" represents spiritual warfare, authority, and persistence.

Why the Enemy Attempts Detainment

The enemy understands spiritual realities far more than many believers do. Keep these truths in mind:

† The devil knows that God is faithful (Deut. 7:9).
† He knows that God answers prayer (Jer. 33:3).
† He knows that faith moves mountains (Mark 11:23).
† He knows that God can do all things (Luke 1:37).
† He knows that God delights in blessing His children (Psalm 35:27).
† He knows God will withhold no good thing from the upright (Psalm 84:11).

- † He knows that you are heir with Christ (Romans 8:17).
- † He knows he cannot manipulate God's will (Job 42:2).
- † He knows God supplies every need (Philippians 4:19).
- † And so he watches closely, seeking unguarded moments (1 Peter 5:8).

Here comes the enemy with a new strategy of detainment.

God does not wait decades before He answers your cry.

So here comes the devil with yet another game plan, to detain your blessing. The blessings have already left heaven in response to your prayers. The breakthrough has been deployed to meet you at the very point of your need. God has issued the supplies, and He has dispatched an angel with the answer on the very first day you asked Him (Daniel 10:12).

God does not wait decades before He answers your cry. He does not require you to undergo ritualistic self-punishment or religious gymnastics before He blesses you. The moment you believe in Jesus Christ as your personal Lord and Savior, you are positioned as a son (John 1:12). And the implication of sonship is profound—it means you have been born into the royal family of God.

As a son, you are immediately and automatically qualified, by the redemptive work of the blood of Jesus, to access blessings and benefits granted by salvation (Ephesians 1:3). Yet, tragically, within Christendom there are countless stories of believers who have prayed, fasted, and done everything within reach to secure certain blessings from God, but the result still seems distant. Many wait, pray, hope, and trust—yet nothing appears to change.

This is the point where discouragement begins its slow creep, even among faith-based and faith-professing believers. The Book of Proverbs declares, *"Hope deferred maketh the heart sick"* (Proverbs 13:12). And today, the Body of Christ is filled with men and women wrestling with despair, hopelessness, frustration, and spiritual fatigue. Their faith and trust in God have been challenged by the spirit of detention.

It is my goal in this chapter to unfold the enemy's strategy—how he seeks to frustrate the life of a believer by *detaining* what God has released. I am confident that after reading this chapter, you will rise with renewed fire—determined to go after the enemy with every ounce of power, anointing, and faith you have in Christ, in order to retrieve everything that has been kept in illegal custody by the spirit of detention (Mark 3:27).

Daniel Syndrome

Daniel was a rare breed of his time.

Daniel was a man of prayer—distinguished, disciplined, and spiritually attuned. In Babylon, he was sought after to solve the impossible. He could read the mysterious handwriting on the wall (Daniel 5:25-28), recall forgotten dreams (Daniel 2:26-28), and interpret visions with precision. Daniel was no ordinary man; he understood the paths of the spirit and moved with the awareness of heavenly realities. His consecration was so deep that it enabled him to defy royal decrees when they violated spiritual purity (Daniel 1:8). Lions could not touch him; angels were his acquaintances (Daniel 6:22).

It was this same Daniel who sought the face of God concerning a matter of national urgency. He understood spiritual access and alignment with heaven. Scripture tells us Daniel sought an answer through *mourning* for three full weeks. Hear his own testimony:

"I ate no pleasant bread, neither came flesh nor wine into my mouth, neither did I anoint myself at all, till three whole weeks were fulfilled" (Daniel 10:3). This statement reveals the weight of what he was dealing with. Daniel deliberately chose a 21-day fast to gain understanding and a response from heaven. Because of his consecration and insight into spiritual realities, Daniel understood the importance of atmosphere, sensitivity, and separation. He was determined to obtain an answer from God, and so he sought it through groaning, prayer, and fasting.

Nothing happened from the first day through the twentieth day.

Imagine the pain.

Imagine the groaning.

Imagine waiting and hearing nothing—no voice, no sign, no whisper, no indication that your prayer is causing even the faintest wave in the realm of the Spirit. Just think about it.

I don't know about you, but I have walked through seasons where heaven felt unbearably far—where nothing moved, the atmosphere grew cold, and the clouds felt impenetrable. I felt frustrated, tormented by the enemy's whispers, reminding me of my past and trying to convince me that God would not hear my prayers anymore. Saints of God, beware of the accuser (Revelation 12:10). His lies are designed to deny you what rightfully belongs to you. But Apostle Paul assures us, *"There is therefore now no condemnation to them which are in Christ Jesus"* (Romans 8:1).

My resilience in prayer proved the enemy wrong. I turned my supplication into warfare—releasing arrows and spiritual missiles, attacking lying spirits with the power of the Word of God (Jeremiah 23:29). And once the devil realizes he is dealing with the wrong person, he withdraws, for the light of the Word exposes his deception and destroys his agenda.

Daniel did not "receive an answer" on day one or day twenty-one—*in the natural*. But spiritually, an intense battle had erupted. This is often the case in our own experiences. The enemy is working against someone right now concerning the very thing you are trusting God for. Do not give up. Your prayers have been answered, and your blessing has already been released. Some matters require separation—a time of pushing away the plate and seeking God with urgency and intensity. Some people retreat to the prayer mountain, others shut themselves in a room, turn off their phones, unplug from social media, and remove every distraction to seek the face of God. I recommend such measures when dealing with weighty matters. I would rather spend 21 days fasting and seeking God than spend 21 years wandering, frustrated, disgraced, and confused.

Your next 21 days may be critical to your next dimension.

Be Aware of Territorial Powers

There are mysteries that lie beyond the veil of human sight—depths untouched by science, regions unmapped by technology. Our ignorance or minimal understanding of the spiritual realm has become a great liability to many. This is not an accusation, nor a blade meant to wound; it is simply a sober truth. For though science has answered many questions, and technology has solved countless human challenges, there remain battles, burdens, and seasons of darkness that no invention of man can remedy. When the wisdom of men reaches its limit, when logic, medicine, and machinery fail, the human heart instinctively turns toward the path of the Spirit, seeking answers only God can reveal : *"Call unto Me, and I will answer thee, and show thee great and mighty things, which thou knowest not"* (Jeremiah 33:3).

Territorial Powers and Spiritual Governance

Daniel sought such answers. His life becomes a lens through which we understand the invisible warfare surrounding our world. When he prayed, an answer was dispatched immediately from heaven, yet a territorial power—the prince of Persia—resisted the messenger for twenty-one days until Michael intervened (Daniel 10:12–13). This single encounter unveils a truth many still overlook: **Territories Are Governed by Spirits**. *There are no empty lands.* Every region, every city, every nation lies under some form of spiritual administration—either godly or demonic (Ephesians 6:12). I have often taught that high-ranking demonic entities known as principalities and powers patrol and influence territories. Believers may pray long and fervently, yet results appear absent because hostile spirits barricade the passage of answers, breakthroughs, and divine intervention. I speak not theoretically. I have personally witnessed the pressure, the resistance, the weight of these beings during intense moments of prayer. Have you ever felt your prayers striking a ceiling and returning empty? Have you sensed yourself praying against a wall of stone? If so, the problem may not be your faith but a territorial spirit resisting your ascent.

In such moments, you must adjust your spiritual strategy—addressing, confronting, and dislodging the powers that frustrate prayer and hinder divine access (Mark 3:27; 2 Corinthians 10:3-5).

The Withholding Spirit

The word *withhold* speaks of restraining something that is rightly due, refusing to release what belongs to another. Yet Scripture reveals a profound assurance: God does not withhold good from His children.

> "For the Lord God is a sun and shield; The Lord will give grace and glory; No good thing will He withhold from those who walk uprightly."(Psalm 84:11).The wise man strengthens this truth: "Withhold not good from them to whom it is due, when it is in the power of your hand to do it." (Proverbs 3:27)

Therefore, anything that is rightfully yours—your blessing, your joy, your breakthrough, your advancement—if withheld, it is not God restraining it. Heaven is not the one delaying you. God is generous, liberal, extravagant in kindness (James 1:17). So who is the withholder? The adversary. The thief. The one Jesus described as coming *"to steal, kill, and destroy"* (John 10:10).

† He withholds answers.
† He blocks doors.
† He delays destinies.
† He frustrates prayers.
† He manipulates time.

But the greater question is this: will you allow him? Christ has already given you authority to trample upon serpents and scorpions and over *all* the power of the enemy (Luke 10:19). The question now is not whether the devil withholds—but whether you will rise in revelation to reclaim what is yours.

What Happened to Daniel?

Daniel prayed within a territory overshadowed by a high-ranking demonic principality known as *the Prince of Persia* (Daniel 10:12–13). His experience unveils a profound spiritual mystery, and to understand it clearly, we must examine the details with precision:

1. Daniel fasted and prayed for twenty-one days (Daniel 10:2–3).
2. Daniel was heard on the very first day he set his heart to seek understanding (Daniel 10:12).
3. Daniel was unaware of the territorial powers influencing the realm where he prayed.
4. Though taken captive into the Babylonian empire, the kingdom had shifted into the Medo-Persian rule, placing him under a new spiritual administration.

5. Daniel continued praying for something God had already provided.
6. Daniel did not know about the spiritual commotion occurring due to his prayer.
7. He was unaware of the angelic warfare between Michael the Archangel and the Prince of Persia (Daniel 10:13, 21).
8. He did not know that the answer to his prayer was detained in transit.
9. He became physically exhausted during his long wait (Daniel 10:8, 17).
10. He did not know that the angel sent with his breakthrough had been resisted and delayed.

How many believers repeat this same painful cycle today? Still asking God to do what has already been done. Still waiting for what Heaven has already released. Still walking away from promises because of ignorance, not absence.

Just because you do not see it does not mean God has not provided it. Just because it has not manifested does not mean it is not already yours. Many have abandoned blessings Heaven released long ago simply because they did not discern the warfare surrounding them. *"It is high time to awake out of sleep"* (Romans 13:11).

Legitimacy to Detain

Before understanding Daniel's delay, we must ask a foundational question: Why was Daniel's answer detained?

In the natural realm, no one can be detained without cause. Likewise, in the spiritual realm, demonic powers cannot legally intercept angelic operations without a legal right or spiritual foothold. Why did the Prince of Persia have the boldness to resist a messenger from God? What "probable cause" gave him jurisdiction? To answer this, we must look at Daniel's name.

The Power of Names

Daniel means "God is my Judge." Biblically, names are not mere labels; they are spiritual identities, prophetic declarations, and legal signatures in the unseen realm.

† God changed Abram's name to Abraham to change his destiny (Genesis 17:5).
† Nabal's wife said his name defined his character (1 Samuel 25:25).
† Jesus' very name carried His divine mission (Matthew 1:21).

Daniel's original name enthroned God's authority over his life. But when he was taken to Babylon—a system steeped in idolatry, sorcery, and demonic rituals—the king imposed upon him a new name as part of their indoctrination. Daniel became Belteshazzar, meaning, "Bel protect his life."

This renaming was not cultural courtesy. It was a spiritual rebranding, a demonic attempt to claim ownership and jurisdiction over Daniel's identity. Babylon's name-changing protocol acted as a ritual of spiritual adoption. It opened a portal that gave the Babylonian realm a degree of oversight over Daniel's activities.

Thus:

† When Daniel prayed as *Daniel*, Heaven recognized him.

† When he lived under the name *Belteshazzar*, the territorial spirit of Persia claimed legal involvement.

Every time Daniel prayed, spiritual realms contended to determine whose authority he truly carried. Daniel's answer was detained because his Babylonian name provided the Prince of Persia with a legal technicality—a foothold enabling temporary resistance. This is the spiritual legality behind the delay.

What Is the Meaning of Your Name?

Do believers today name their children recklessly? Sadly, yes.

Years ago, a young mother brought her son for dedication in our church. When I saw the name she intended to give him, something stirred within me. Upon inquiry, I was shocked to discover that the name simply meant "goat." She had no idea. When I explained the meaning and urged her to choose a biblical name instead, she agreed—and peace followed.

Some may dismiss this truth through intellectual or theological arguments, but Scripture shows us repeatedly that the spiritual realm operates on principles that the natural mind cannot fully grasp.

Names carry identity, authority, and spiritual weight. In the unseen realm, your name speaks before you do.

Angelic Intervention

God's government is hierarchical in both structure and operation, for He is a God of perfect order (1 Corinthians 14:40). From eternity, He designed the celestial realm with precision—angelic beings crafted with unique features, functions, and ranks. These messengers of light are not ornamental figures of heaven; they are servants of the Most High, commissioned to minister to the heirs of salvation (Hebrews 1:14).

Each angel carries an assignment. Each assignment carries a weight. Each weight carries a divine purpose.

Angels engage in warfare, deliver messages, carry verdicts, execute judgments, and escort blessings from the throne of God into the hands of men. They are Heaven's swift winds, Heaven's flames of fire (Psalm 104:4), running with divine intelligence from the courts of glory to the earth below.

It was Gabriel, Heaven's herald, who broke the silence of centuries when he stood before Zechariah, announcing the coming of John the Baptist, *"your prayer is heard"* (Luke 1:13-19). The same Gabriel carried the most sacred announcement in history—the Immaculate Conception of Jesus Christ—declaring to Mary, *"The Holy Ghost shall come upon thee..."* (Luke 1:26-35).

It was an angelic host that filled the night sky over Bethlehem, proclaiming the birth of the Savior to shepherds keeping watch (Luke 2:8-14). It was an angel who met trembling Gideon beneath the oak, revealing Heaven's strategy to overthrow the Midianite oppression and restore Israel's dignity (Judges 6:11-16). It was an angel who appeared to Manoah's barren wife, foretelling the birth of Samson, a deliverer formed by divine instruction (Judges 13:3–5).

From Genesis to Revelation, the footprints of angelic activity are unmistakable. They ascend and descend upon the affairs of men, engaging in battles, delivering messages, protecting destinies, and enforcing the decrees of the Almighty.

The Scriptures testify that angels walk among us more often than we discern, urging us to entertain strangers with humility, *"for thereby some have entertained angels unawares"* (Hebrews 13:2). In every age, every dispensation, and every crisis, Heaven has never been without its agents. Where God sends a word, angels carry it. Where God releases a blessing, angels escort it. Where God initiates warfare, angels enforce His victory.

Their involvement is not ancient history—it is an ongoing reality in the life of every believer who walks in alignment with Heaven's rhythm.

Angelic Encounters

Personally, I have encountered angels on several occasions. Let me share with you one such moment—an encounter witnessed by many.

We had entered a season of fasting that lasted thirty days. Each day, we gathered at the church at 6:00 p.m. to close out in prayer. On the final day of the fast, as I was driving to the church, the Spirit of God spoke to me, saying, *"Son, I will show you a sign tonight."* I felt His presence settle around me like a warm mantle. I did not know what to expect, but deep within, I sensed that our sacrifice of fasting and prayer had risen as a sweet aroma before the Lord (Psalm 141:2).

When I arrived at the church, I joyfully announced to the brethren what the Lord had spoken. We began with worship, and praise ascended toward heaven like incense. The atmosphere grew thick—tangible with the glory of God.

As was customary, one of my leaders brought a bottle of water and poured half of it into a silver cup, placing both items on a latch attached to the pulpit. As we prayed, I suddenly found myself before a throne. I was overwhelmed, enveloped in the radiant aura of God's presence. My hands gripped the edge of the pulpit as my body trembled under the power of the Holy Spirit. Tears streamed freely as the sanctuary echoed with cries of *"Glory! Glory! Glory!"*

The pulpit shook beneath the weight of the anointing. I heard the silver cup fall—and the bottle tumble to the floor. But I cared nothing for the cup or the water at that moment. My spirit was lost in worship. Yet I sensed a presence—someone near me—moving, adjusting, touching. Irritated, I assumed a member of the church was more concerned with spilled water than the holy visitation taking place. Determined to correct the distraction, I opened my eyes, but no one was there.

The congregation remained bowed in worship, lost in tears and reverent adoration. Yet to my astonishment, the silver cup was back on the latch, the bottle stood beside it, and both were filled—*exactly as before.* Only the water on the floor testified that something had indeed fallen. When the prayer concluded, I asked who had placed the cup and bottle back. Every person testified that they had been on their knees or faces before the Lord, weeping and worshiping. At that moment, the Spirit reminded me of His words earlier that day: *"I will show you a sign tonight."*

I invited everyone to the pulpit. Together we saw the water still on the floor, the cup filled again, the bottle restored. Everything had been divinely set back in order. We erupted into worship once more. And yes—I drank that water with joy, for it was indeed water touched by heaven. The silver cup became consecrated, a vessel of remembrance, and it remains in the Ark of Covenant in our prayer room to this day.

I know this may sound strange to some, but angels have always interacted with humanity. Scripture affirms their constant involvement:

- † They minister to the heirs of salvation (Hebrews 1:14).
- † They deliver divine messages (Luke 1:26–38).
- † They protect God's people (Psalm 91:11).
- † They engage in heavenly warfare (Revelation 12:7–9).
- † They guide and strengthen believers in moments of crisis (Acts 12:7–11).

Angels are real—more real than many perceive. They walk beside us, battle for us, defend us, and carry out the will of God concerning our lives.

Daniel, too, encountered such an angel—one who unveiled the truth behind his delayed answer. Though Daniel's prayer was heard on the first day he sought the Lord, the messenger sent with his answer was detained by the prince of Persia, a territorial principality, until Michael, the great archangel, intervened (Daniel 10:12–13).

Daniel continued praying, unaware that his blessing was *already released* and simply *held up in transit*. Many believers are the same today, still petitioning heaven for what God has already provided, unaware that the delay is a matter of warfare, not unwillingness.

Daniel's story did not end without an answer, yet precious time was still lost, and time recoils from anything that wastes its worth. Some may argue that the victory alone matters, and yes, we rejoice with Daniel; but we also feel the sting of detention—the frustration, the uncertainty, the weight of being held back. This is our lesson: for some of us, a single lost day can feel like a decade carved from our destiny. We don't need not endure what is avoidable. We don't need to sit in silent hope while refusing the changes that invite breakthrough. Your life is too sacred, too intentionally crafted by God to be surrendered to chance or the trembling hands of probability.

4

THE SPIRIT OF DIVERSION

We are God's best product...

Let me begin this chapter by reminding us that we are powerful people made in the image and likeness of a powerful God. We are God's best product, and nothing in creation, both visible and invisible, can come close to the distinctive qualities and uniqueness exclusively endowed upon man. Looking at the various ways that the enemy is using to take away blessings must be a turning point. Our lives must become better, and the days ahead of us are far better than the days behind us. The end goal of this book is to teach you the strategies that you need in order to recover everything that the enemy has stolen from you. So far, we have seen the strategies of the enemy in an attempt to deny you what God has freely given to you in Christ. Let us explore further in this chapter another strategy of the enemy against believers today—it is called the spirit of diversion.

God's plan is that you shall be blessed in every aspect of your life. Your spiritual prosperity is God's primary goal when He sent His only begotten Son to die on the cross for your sin. This accounts for the kind of relationship that God wants to keep with you, and in such a relationship, He has already meted out measures of blessings for you pertaining to life and godliness. When we stand before God in prayer, we are connected with Him through our relationship that is intimately strengthened through obedience and total dependency on Him. Everything else is built on the bedrock of our closeness with Him. We are both strong and fruitful as we remain in Him. In the Gospel of John chapter 15, Jesus reminded us that our fruitfulness and prosperity are contingent on remaining in Him. Paul told the church of Ephesus to *"be strong in the Lord and in the power of His might"* (Ephesians 6:10).

The point I am trying to make is that we must maintain an unbroken line of relationship with God through our prayers, worship, uprightness, and daily walk with Him so as to keep the inflow of His constant blessings coming to us from above. Notice that the hand that gives is always on top of the receiving hand, but there must be alignment to avoid the gift falling into another place. Here is another strategy that the enemy is using to manipulate believers out of their God-given blessings; again, it is called the spirit of diversion.

Diversion is "the turning aside of something from its intended course." Words such as rerouting, deflection, and misdirection reveal the manner in which these spirits operate.

A letter misplaced in a mailbox may cause needless sorrow and delay. The rightful owner may wait anxiously, not knowing that the contents therein were of utmost urgency. Even so, countless blessings—jobs, promotions, financial release, opportunities—have been diverted to another.

Some have lost contracts to the unworthy. Promotions have been granted by bias or corruption. Students deserving honor have been replaced by those less qualified. The world may deem you unworthy, but divine purpose overthrows human judgment. When Saul was anointed king, the people cried, "Is Saul also among the prophets?"—a question born from doubt and human evaluation. Yet God alone is the one who lifts one up and humbles another. Likewise, when Philip spoke of Jesus, Nathanael asked, "Can any good thing come out of Nazareth?" Humanity judges carnally; God chooses sovereignly

What do you do when what belongs to you is diverted to another? The world and human standards have already discounted many as being unworthy or below pedigree and unfit for sudden crowns. We live in a world of racial prejudice, gender inequality, and cultural discrimination. You cannot change the world system or what people think about you, but you can change the way you think about yourself.

Jacob, Joseph, Manasseh, and Ephraim

In the 48th chapter of the book of Genesis, Joseph had two sons, Manasseh and Ephraim. I want you to watch closely how the spirit of diversion operates. Jacob, we are told, was old and going blind, and Joseph wanted his father to speak prophetically and bless his two sons before he died. Therefore, he brought his two boys, Manasseh, being the firstborn, on his left hand toward his father's right hand, and Ephraim on his right hand toward Jacob's left hand. This was deliberately arranged according to human standard, culture, and tradition. However, Jacob placed his right hand on Ephraim's head, the less and unlikely one to receive such a blessing from the patriarch instead of Manasseh, the firstborn. *"And Israel stretched out his right hand and laid it upon Ephraim's head, who was the younger, and his left hand upon Manasseh's head, guiding his hands wittingly"* (Genesis 48:14). Joseph had his own preference, but God's plan and providence always prevail. Manasseh was the popular, charismatic, eloquent, and people's choice, but God chose Ephraim. When Joseph saw his father's right hand coming upon Ephraim's head, it displeased him, and he held up his father's hand to remove it from Ephraim's head to Manasseh's head. Joseph quickly tried to divert the hand of blessing and breakthrough from Ephraim to Manasseh. Just pause and think about this.

Joseph was displaced on the account that God chose a less-qualified person over the popular one. God has chosen you for that position, and nothing will change it in Jesus' name. Your promotion will not be diverted to another. The spirit of diversion is rooted in envy, hatred, discrimination, intimidation, jealousy, corruption, ridicule, demeaning others, and so on. Some can testify how the spirit of diversion has denied them opportunities that God gave to them. You must not allow your God-given blessings to be diverted to another. You must stand your ground. You must use your voice to advocate for yourself. You must speak, because in the realm of the Spirit, silence equals consent. You may have been swindled, scammed, ridiculed, or even intimidated out of what rightfully belongs to you. In this season, you must take what belongs to you by force and refuses to be deprived any longer.

How to Contend with the Spirit of Diversion

You must know when the enemy is playing into your gallery. Jacob did not yield to the opposing hand of Joseph because he stood his ground and blessed Ephraim over Manasseh. You must learn to stand your ground, break the hand of the strong man, and take what belongs to you by force. You must refuse to be trampled under by the agent of the enemy in human form because Jesus gave you authority over them. The Bible says that they are under your feet. Therefore, as a child of God, pull everything down—imaginations, intimidations, conspiracy, discriminations—and be bold as a lion in doing so. Declare with authority that God's blessings are mine, and none shall take it away from me.

Declarations:
- † Let the blessings come down on me.
- † Let the blessing rain down on me.
- † Let the blessing shine on me.
- † Let the blessing blow around me.
- † Let the blessing overshadow me from the North, South, East, and West.
- † Let the blessing of God come upon me. I am blessed forever! Hallelujah, Hallelujah, Hallelujah!

Power of Declaration

Whatever you believe you are given power to become.

Whatever you believe, you are given the power to become. Your faith in God is colossal, vast, and varied in application. I have had the privilege of meeting people at various degrees in their faith. I have come across people that have extreme faith in the redeeming power of the blood of Jesus Christ. The same people with such faith expression are not able to access the blessings of God available to them. Faith in redemption is no different from faith in reception and recovery because whatever man lost—spiritually, physically, and materially—was all recovered through the same act of redemption on the cross of Calvary.

The knowledge of salvation in its entirety is very important for a life of victory. Apostle Peter captured this concept in his second epistle when he wrote, *"According as His divine power hath given unto us all things that pertain unto life and godliness, through the knowledge of Him that hath called us to glory and virtue"* (2 Peter 1:3). Notice that all things have been given to us, but it requires a depth of knowledge to access it and to declare it. Declaration, therefore, is a function of knowledge.

Your Words Create Your World

Faith has no value without a voice.

The writer of the book of Hebrews confirmed that *"through faith we understand that the worlds were framed by the word of God, so that things which are seen were not made of things which do appear"* (Hebrews 11:3). Words are powerful because they are alive and have the ability to activate the forces that make things happen. Nothing happens until something is spoken, and faith has no value without a voice.

In Genesis chapter one verse three, nothing ever appeared until God spoke. It is your faith that gives you a voice, and where there is a voice, there is also a force. Therefore, create your world with your words, because it is the principle of creation and it never changes.

Speak out your blessings today: bless your children, your household, your congregation, your business, your marriage, your career, your ministry, your city, and everything around you. Declare it openly that the ends of the earth may hear you. Give your faith a voice and your world will look different—*"We having the same spirit of faith, according as it is written, I believed, and therefore have I spoken; we also believe, and therefore speak"* (2 Corinthians 4:13).

Speak as a commander and declare as follows:
- † I am redeemed.
- † I am healed.
- † I am set free.
- † I am blessed and not cursed.
- † I am above and not beneath.
- † I am favored.
- † I am prosperous.

Let the mountains and the hills hear your voice, that today and forever, your blessing shall not be diverted in Jesus' name. My blessing shall locate me in Jesus' name. Speak and keep speaking, for this is your season of prophetic declaration.

5

THE SPIRIT OF DECEPTION

A new birth experience is about moving from one kingdom to another. In order to enter into a new kingdom from the old, certain gateways must be opened. Gateways are the means through which one can experience the benefits of that kingdom. Obviously—and spiritually speaking—there are many gateways in a spiritually recreated human being. As members of this kingdom, God begins by opening our eyes to the reality of His Kingdom. The regeneration experience begins by allowing us to see the kingdom that we are now a part of. This is why the eye-gate is the first gate to be opened.

Jesus told Nicodemus that kingdom membership comes through the new birth experience. This experience brings exposure to spiritual realities. The kingdom opens our ability to see its realm and activities, creating in us the desire to enter. *"Except a man be born again, he cannot see the kingdom of God."* Notice that Jesus' explanation of this process began with eyesight. This is very important to our subject. Jesus then continued His explanation of what happens after the kingdom is seen: *"Verily, verily, I say unto thee, except a man be born of water and of the Spirit, he cannot enter into the kingdom of God."*

Let us look at these closely: First, the born-again experience begins with the ability to see the kingdom of God. Secondly, the born-again experience continues as the believer enters and walks into the kingdom of God. The question is: *Why is this important, and how is it related to our topic?*

Spiritual Consciousness

The Bible is a book containing many stories because whatever was written was meant for us to learn from, develop by, and integrate into our daily walk with God. God is unchanging in both nature and principles; therefore, Apostle Paul wrote, *"For whatsoever things were written aforetime were written for our learning, that we through patience and comfort of the scriptures might have hope"* (Romans 15:4).

In Paul's reasoning, the stories of men and women who encountered God were carefully documented to give us the opportunity to learn—so that we can follow their good examples for similar success or learn from their mistakes so we can avoid repeating their failures and troubles. Based on this, we can look back in time and observe several examples that can help us in dealing with the spirit of deception.

No matter the assignment God has for a man or a woman, a certain degree of awareness and spiritual consciousness must be in place for fulfillment. God invested time and space in Scripture to educate us on the modus operandi of the devil—his nature as a fallen angel and his goal as an adversary. We cannot live in a dangerous world as though everything is well. On the contrary, things are getting worse by the day.

Apostle Peter wrote in his epistle about the need for the Christian soldier to be conscious of the rampage of the enemy, whom he identified as an adversary and likened to a roaring lion seeking whom he may devour.

- † Adversary: One's opponent in conflict or dispute.
- † Roaring lion: A territorial sound used by a dominant male to announce his presence—symbolizing intimidation and fear.
- † Seeking: Attempting to obtain something in a desperate manner—symbolizing determination and viciousness.
- † Prowling: Moving restlessly and steadily in search of prey—symbolizing rage, aggression, and vengeance.

Nothing, in my opinion, should give the Christian soldier more awakening than these words, which reveal the ministry and personality of the opponent we contend with daily. Peter therefore began with a call to spiritual consciousness, awareness, awakening, and alertness by admonishing us to be:

- † "Sober": not affected by any harmful influence; clear-minded and free from interference.
- † "Alert": a military expression used in emergencies, meaning to pay full attention and be ready because danger is near.
- † "Vigilant": keeping careful watch for possible dangers or difficulties.

The summary of the above scripture is a clarion call for the Body of Christ to rise from slumber because the devil is actively on his diabolical assignment: *"Wherefore he saith, awake thou that sleepest, and arise from the dead, and Christ shall give thee light"* (Ephesians 5:14). Notice how Paul uses a metaphor to illustrate the degree of unconsciousness in a believer who refuses the call to sobriety. Such a believer is like a dead person—totally unaware of his surroundings, incapable of reacting regardless of the mutilation done to his lifeless body. The answer, according to Apostle Paul, is the light, which is Christ, "the hope of glory." In John chapter 1, Jesus Christ is presented as both the Word and the Light. The power of light is its ability to overcome darkness. In this context, light symbolizes awareness, understanding, and enlightenment, while darkness represents ignorance, concealment, and bondage.

Consider the following scriptures:

† *"But while men slept, his enemy came and sowed tares among the wheat, and went his way"* (Matthew 13:25).
† *"Lest Satan should take advantage of us, for we are not ignorant of his devices"* (2 Corinthians 2:11).
† *"But I fear, lest by any means, as the serpent beguiled Eve through his subtlety, so your minds should be corrupted from the simplicity that is in Christ"* (2 Corinthians 11:3).
† *"And no marvel; for Satan himself is transformed into an angel of light"* (2 Corinthians 11:14).

These scriptures, and many others, point to the topic at hand: the spirit of deception.

Deception

By definition, deception is the action of deceiving someone. To accomplish this, the deceiver employs words, actions, distractions, or even inaction. Many tools exist in the world to deceive people. Many have been turned into merchandise through:

† scams
† trickery
† manipulation
† lies
† forgery
† false promises

But above all deceivers stands the devil, whom Scripture describes as *subtle, crafty, and cunning*. Deception thrives where ignorance abounds. One cannot deceive a person who is well-informed. This is why Apostle Paul reminded us that Eve was deceived, but Adam disobeyed. Deception works through ignorance; disobedience works through rebellion. The devil preys on people in two ways:

1. Deception, through ignorance
2. Disobedience, through rebellion

To defeat the devil, the believer must be:

† sober
† enlightened
† well-informed
† spiritually aware
† understanding
† growing in knowledge

† knowledgeable about both the Creator and the creature
† spiritually conscious

Victory over deception begins with spiritual awareness.

The Spirit of Deception in the Garden of Eden

"Adam, where are you?" This question still echoes loudly in the mind of every man or woman in a fallen state. Anyone who has become a victim of the tactical maneuvers of the devil through deception is still confronted with this unending question—*Where are you?*

Beyond one's immediate physical location, God's question addresses the state of the mind. In other words, *how connected is your mind to its spiritual surroundings?* Whenever God asks a question concerning any area of our lives, His goal is always to awaken a level of consciousness necessary for His imminent intervention.

God does not ask questions out of ignorance—certainly not a God whose intelligence is superior and whose knowledge is unsearchable. His questions are designed to provoke readiness in us for what He is about to do in our situation. Therefore, "Adam, where are you?" was not a question of location, but of position.

The same inquiry is being asked of us today: Where is your position in the Kingdom? Are you aware of what is happening around you?

The Significance of Eden

God placed man in the garden to manage and cultivate it. Eden was not merely a physical garden; it was a place of spiritual connection. God's meeting place and His fellowship with man occurred in Eden. Adam named every animal *from* the garden. Vital decisions that shaped humanity's destiny were made in the garden.

Eden was Heaven's embassy on Earth.

As stated earlier, God planted Eden with intentionality and purpose. Lucifer understood the significance of Eden before he appeared there. His ambition, greed, and corrupt desire had already been exposed, and his determination remained relentless: *"Thou hast been in Eden, the garden of God... every precious stone was thy covering."*

Eden was strategic for the execution of any agenda—whether God's, man's, or the devil's. This explains why all three had vested interest in the garden. Whoever controlled Eden influenced what happened in the entire world. That truth is profound. Lucifer attempted to project his hidden, insidious agenda in the Garden of God, but failed. What he could not accomplish in God's garden, he sought to achieve in man's garden. To ensure success, he employed a creature compatible with his nature and mission: *"Now the serpent was more subtle than any beast of the field which the Lord God had made."*

By choosing the serpent, he revealed his intentions and his personality. Subtle implies:
- † craftiness
- † hidden motives

† deceitful strategies
† indirect methods

This embodies the entire goal of the spirit of deception.

The Enemy's Character and Ongoing Influence

We are dealing with an enemy who is highly intelligent. God gave him wisdom, but he allowed it to become corrupted through pride, selfishness, jealousy, and hypocrisy. Do we not see these characteristics every day in our world? Is not the world today infiltrated with these same attributes? Although the tools used to carry out deception may differ across generations, the goal is always the same. Faces may differ, cultures may differ, and methods may differ, but the spirit behind them remains consistent. Adam and Eve became victims of this spirit—and so do many people today.

The Law of Association and Assimilation

The law of association inevitably leads to the law of assimilation, which simply means: You become what you consistently associate with.

It was in the Garden of Eden that Lucifer, through his craftiness, succeeded in attacking our first parents by convincing Eve to eat from the forbidden tree. The mystery of the tree is not the main concern here. Simply put, eating from it amounted to rebellion and disobedience—contrary to false claims that God set a trap for man. Scripture makes it clear: "God does not tempt any man with evil, neither is He tempted by evil."

Unfortunately, Adam and Eve fell victim to the spirit of deception. As a consequence, humanity lost everything freely given by God. Satan even boasted of this loss during the temptation of Jesus: *"All this power will I give thee, and the glory of them: for that is delivered unto me; and to whomsoever I will I give it. If thou therefore wilt worship me, all shall be thine."* (Luke 4:6–7).

Can you hear his arrogance? "To whomsoever I will…" "If thou wilt worship me…" Satan still sets conditions for his victims today. He demands worship before he gives anything. Nothing destroys the soul more than idolatry. Many people have pledged, and even surrendered, their souls to Satan for mere trinkets.

Quid Pro Quo in the Kingdom of Darkness

Nothing the devil offers is ever free. Everything operates on a principle of quid pro quo—*this for that*. Satan demands something valuable in exchange for whatever he promises. Anyone who approaches the kingdom of darkness must understand that the cost is always greater than the benefit. This is why Jesus asked: "What shall it profit a man if he gains the whole world and loses his soul?"

Many today are willing to trade their eternal destiny for temporary satisfaction, ignoring the spiritual consequences. Once the soul becomes the currency of negotiation, deception has already succeeded.

The Explosion of Knowledge and the Rise of Deception

We are living in an age marked by an unprecedented explosion of knowledge—technological, scientific, and philosophical. However, with this increase there has also come a flood of misinformation, distorted truths, and cleverly packaged lies. The enemy exploits this generation's hunger for advancement by disguising deception as enlightenment.

People now embrace ideas that contradict Scripture simply because they appear intelligent, progressive, or logical. Truth is being redefined, morality is being reshaped, and spirituality is becoming diluted. The enemy's most effective weapon in this age is intellectual deception disguised as wisdom.

Daniel prophesied this era when he said, "Knowledge shall increase." But he also implied that discernment must increase with it.

Unfortunately, many have grown intellectually sharp but spiritually dull.

The Spirit of Deception in the Last Days

The spirit of deception is not coming—it is already here, operating with greater intensity than ever before. Jesus warned that in the last days, deception would be so sophisticated that even the elect *could* be deceived if they are not vigilant.

Consider the characteristics of this end-time deception:

† It appeals to emotions rather than truth.
† It disguises itself as spirituality, offering supernatural experiences detached from God's Word.
† It promotes self-worship, encouraging people to become the ultimate standard of truth.
† It mixes light with darkness, making it harder to identify error.
† It destroys moral foundations, causing confusion where conviction once stood.

The enemy knows his time is short; therefore, he intensifies his efforts to drag as many souls as possible into darkness.

A Call to Discernment and Spiritual Awareness

The same question God asked Adam is being asked of this generation: "Where are you?"

† Where is your spiritual awareness?
† Where is your conviction?
† Where is your fellowship with God?
† Where is your identity in the Kingdom?

To overcome deception, believers must:

1. *Remain rooted in Scripture.* Stay planted in the eternal Word, for *"man shall not live by bread alone, but by every word that proceeds from the mouth of God"* (Matthew 4:4). Let Scripture be the anchor of your soul and the lamp for your feet (Psalm 119:105).

2. *Nurture a consistent prayer life.* Cultivate communion with God, for prayer is the breath of

the believer. *"Pray without ceasing"* (1 Thessalonians 5:17) and draw near with confidence to the throne of grace (Hebrews 4:16).

3. *Guard their minds from subtle influences.* Watch over the gates of your thoughts, for the enemy works through whispers. *"Be transformed by the renewing of your mind"* (Romans 12:2) and take every thought captive to the obedience of Christ (2 Corinthians 10:5).

4. *Submit to the Holy Spirit's guidance.* Yield to the gentle leading of the Spirit, for *"as many as are led by the Spirit of God, they are the sons of God"* (Romans 8:14). He is the Counselor who guides into all truth (John 16:13).

5. *Walk in humility and obedience.* Tread the narrow path with a humble heart, for God *"gives grace to the humble"* (James 4:6). Obedience is the fragrance of true devotion—*"to obey is better than sacrifice"* (1 Samuel 15:22).

Deception thrives where discernment is absent. The only safe place in these last days is in God's kingdom. Don't be deceived by what is easily enticed to the eyes, for underneath may lie evil and hidden snares. The devil will try everything to deceive many out of their blessings—through falsehood, through fake miracles, and through prophecies that carry no spiritual accountability, no commitment to diligence, and little or no emphasis on godliness and holiness (Matthew 24:24; 2 Corinthians 11:13–14).

Any blessing that does not connect you to the Source of every good and perfect gift is a snare, and you must flee from it like a gazelle escaping the trap of the hunter (James

1:17; Proverbs 6:5). Do not be deceived, for the adversary still prowls around like a roaring lion, seeking whom he may devour (1 Peter 5:8). Hold fast to truth, cling to righteousness, and remain anchored in the light of God's Word, for only then can you discern what is real from what is merely enticing.

We are going to examine closely the final spirit the enemy will deploy in his attempt to interfere with your blessing. Thus far, our eyes have been opened wider to the subtle techniques he uses. At this point, we have become more familiar with his games, and we thank God that we remain vigilant in the spirit (2 Corinthians 2:11; 1 Peter 5:8).

Yet it is deeply important that we never assume the battle is over. The warfare of the believer does not cease simply because one tactic has failed (Ephesians 6:12). If the enemy cannot lure you away from the truth through deception or a lying spirit, he may, in his fury, attempt to deface the blessing itself when he senses that we have grown reluctant, weary, or unwatchful (Matthew 26:41).

Therefore, remain steady. Remain discerning. Remain awake in the spirit, for *"we are not ignorant of his devices"* and the God who watches over you neither slumbers nor sleeps (Psalm 121:4; 2 Corinthians 2:11).

6

THE SPIRIT OF DEFACEMENT

The blessing of the Lord, it maketh rich, and he addeth no sorrow with it (Proverbs 10:22).

Every good gift and every perfect gift is from above, and cometh down from the Father of lights, with whom is no variableness, neither shadow of turning (James 1:17).

Brethren, when the Bible admonishes us to pray without ceasing, and when Jesus Christ told a parable pointing to the necessity of prayer without breaking the cycle, it was insightful and much needed—not only in obtaining answers to our prayers, but in preserving them. This is where most of us become unwatched and retire untimely. Listen: we don't cease from prayer. We don't take a vacation from warfare. Many may think this is becoming increasingly fanatical, but until we understand the mind of the spiritual being we are contending with, our logical approach will always threaten our spiritual victories.

Many individuals have questioned what they perceive to be unanswered prayers from God, either because there are blemishes or unsatisfactory outcomes. The integrity of the above scriptures appears on trial, and the unspeakable joy that fervent prayer is supposed to deliver seems denied. Let's be clear: God is not the author of confusion.

† God is able to finish what He started.
† God has a crowning end to every work of faith.
† God is a prayer-answering God to any man or woman.
† God has a stake in your answered prayers because His glory is exclusive.
† God has the absolute power to perfect everything concerning you (Psalm 138:8).
† God is interested in giving you the abundance of life, joy always, beauty for ashes, and the oil of gladness in exchange for the spirit of heaviness (Isaiah 61:1–3).

Anything short of these is the hidden hand of the enemy. His mission and ministry have not changed (John 10:10). The disciples of Jesus drew His attention to tares growing alongside the wheat. The owner did not plant the tares. So, the question becomes: Who did it? How and when was it planted? Jesus quickly identified the culprit: *"An enemy hath done this"* (Matthew 13:28).

When (the time) the enemy sowed tares is even more interesting, and the answer lies in Jesus' simple response: "While men slept" (Matthew 13:25). A lot can go wrong when we fall into spiritual slumber. "Sleep" here does not mean resting; it suggests a lack of watchfulness, complacency, and the attitude of declaring "It is over" at the height of battle. "While men slept" is an indictment to the Christian soldier who begins to meddle with civilian affairs while still supposedly engaging in active spiritual warfare. This is why Apostle Paul warns us, *"Awake thou that sleepest"* (Ephesians 5:14).

I will never forget the words of my spiritual father, Pastor (Dr.) James Fadel, Chairman of RCCGNA and Continental Overseer/Assistant to our Father in the Lord, God's General, Pastor Enoch Adeboye. I brought a matter to him for counsel. After listening carefully, he gave me word profound of wisdom: "You are praying but not watching." That word still echoes in my spirit and has guided me in my journey, yielding unprecedented results and outcomes.

Watch and Pray

It is important to highlight that we must pray with our spiritual eyes open. There is no rule on praying with eyes physically open or closed. Closing your eyes reduces distractions; opening them spiritually allows visibility, navigation, and precision. Monitoring your spiritual environment for detection and confrontation is important to reduce reprisal attacks to zero. This is where our prayers become most powerful—not only in receiving blessings from God but in ensuring immunity against demonic interference or infiltration.

Remember, the devil always seeks to create bias in the heart of a believer. He wants you to question God's love. He wants you to lose faith and doubt God's character as good. He wants to pollute your mind by sowing seeds of discord to ruin your relationship with God. He is subtle and persistent. One of the ways he attempts this is by defacing God's blessings to you.

To deface means "to spoil the surface or appearance of something," sometimes beyond recognition. The goal is to make the object unappealing. When something loses its attraction, sweetness, or ability to gratify, its value diminishes. How painful it is to wait in hope and prayer, only to feel your waiting was in vain because the outcome seems disappointing.

Unlike Simeon, who waited patiently to see the Messiah, his soul rejoiced and his spirit leaped with joy when he beheld the Christ. His years of hope, uncertainty, mockery, and delay melted away when he held the Messiah. He uttered in gratitude, *"Lord, now lettest thou thy servant depart in peace, for mine eyes have seen thy salvation"* (Luke 2:29-30). Prophecy met time in that holy moment, where Anna, the prophetess, also rejoiced. Perfect is too weak a word to describe the Word made flesh, yet God, in His mercy, came to dwell with us.

When I think of the devil's strategy to smear God's blessings with controversy, my mind races. Many real stories come to mind—miscarriages, deformities, disabilities, wealth without health, terminal diseases that arise after years of effort, and more.

BUT...

This three-letter word can be a maker or a breaker. "But"—a game changer! It can wipe away tears instantly or cause them to flow. It can douse tension or escalate it. A beautiful story can be polluted by this word. It restores hope or destroys it. Many stories end in tragedy with "but," while many end in victory with the same word. May the "but" in your story change for good in Jesus' name!

Consider Naaman.

His pedigree was impeccable. His achievements unmatched. He was a decorated veteran with national honor. Everything about this noble general was admirable—*but he was a leper* (2 Kings 5:1). That one condition overshadowed all his greatness. Leprosy was not only a physical disease; it was also:

† A social disease
† A psychological disease
† An emotional disease

Social Disease. Victims of leprosy were isolated due to its contagiousness. They had to announce their presence, like those during the COVID-19 era, to prevent spreading the disease. The emotional pain was unimaginable. It is one thing for others to discuss your situation—another for you to broadcast your own shame. This is the agenda of the enemy: to use defacement to diminish your blessings.

Psychological Disease. Human beings thrive on acceptance (Maslow's hierarchy of needs). Rejection breeds trauma. Leprosy eats into the mind. Think of this great man—honored, wealthy, successful—yet psychologically wounded. With all your achievements, education, wealth, houses, and awards, are you still lonely inside? Are you battling invisible torment while the world praises you? Is something eating you up while you try to mask the stench with appearance?

"...but he was a leper."

Are you a leper in your wedding gown?

A leper in the boardroom?

A leper behind the pulpit or in the pews?

A leper married to the most honorable spouse?

A leper as the first lady or national leader?

A leper with multiple businesses?

A leper with academic glory?

A leper crowned with earthly beauty or fame?

A leper who is the highest-paid celebrity?

I have good news: God will change your life for good.

Thank God that leprosy symbolizes the spiritual disease Christ bore for us.

"For by His stripes you are healed" (Isaiah 53:5).

Thank God—you are made whole in Christ!

Emotional Disease. Emotional matters dwell beneath the heart of their victims. I have a strong empathy for this subject, partially because I have had a fair share of bleeding—yet still leading. Emotional pain is not alien to men, and the danger of this situation is real. Stories and circumstances, both intra-biblical and extra-biblical, easily attest to this.

In John chapter 4, Jesus met a woman of Samaria by the well of Jacob. She came to draw water with her little pot, at an hour she chose intentionally, so she might avoid running into anyone. Women usually came to the well earlier, and at that same time, shepherds brought their flocks to drink. Often, women met their future husbands at the well. Remember that Abraham's servant met Rebekah at the well; she later became the wife of Isaac. Remember how Moses met Zipporah, who became his wife. Wells were not only places of drawing water, but environments of mingling, divine meetings, and social interactions.

This woman, though appearing outwardly fine, was suffering from emotional leprosy. She masked her emotional pain and the abuse she endured from different men. She became evasive in conversation, exhibiting symptoms of social aggression. Her emotional leprosy was covered, but *nothing is hidden from the eyes of God, "before whom all things are naked and open"* (Hebrews 4:13). At the end, Jesus uncovered her real pain, and she became free. Her testimony was, *"Come, see a man who told me all that I ever did; could this be the Christ?"* (John 4:29). Think about this—from a passive isolationist to an aggressive evangelist!

Many cases are like hers: from abuse, childhood trauma, relationships destroyed by betrayal. People abandoned by earthly fathers often struggle to trust the Heavenly Father.

Think about a woman saying "I do" at the altar to a man who reminds her of her ex. Think about entering business or personal partnership while carrying scars of trust issues. This is what the devil delights in, for one cannot fully enjoy the blessings of the Lord when too many sorrows remain attached (Proverbs 10:22).

How to Secure Your Blessing

God is the beginning and the ending for a reason. We call on Him at the beginning when we need something, but somewhere along the line we abandon Him—as though He is no longer necessary. Our attitude begins to suggest that by our own power and might, we achieved the result ourselves. This is reckless behavior, opening the door to the enemy. God must remain from the beginning to the end through praise, thanksgiving, and honor. He is *"the Author and Finisher of our faith"* (Hebrews 12:2). You must look unto Him throughout your journey—even when everything seems to be working for you.

How to Defeat the Spirit of Defacement

Testimony. Testimony is a very powerful tool of spiritual warfare. Not only does it return glory and honor to God, but it also opens the door for more testimonies. Testimonies expose the devil publicly and disengage his vices from the lives of many. The Scripture declares, *"They overcame him by the blood of the Lamb and by the word of their testimony"* (Revelation 12:11). Testimony begins the moment you bring a matter before God. This is why Apostle Paul admonished us to add thanksgiving to our requests (Philippians 4:6). Thanksgiving obligates God to perform. It is a proactive approach, a strategy in prayer, and an expression of active faith. Testifying that God is ever faithful to His promises and declaring your season of miracles is a solid strategy.

Testimonies perfect blessings and miracles because the outcome stands before many witnesses. Testimonies move God—not only to finish and perfect for one, but to begin or increase for another. I encourage you to come before God and testify of your healing, breakthroughs, sudden turnarounds, and all the miracles the Lord has granted you. Don't be intimidated. Don't wait until everything is done—this is a carnal mindset; spiritually, all things are already done, completed, and perfected. Your testimony demonstrates that you are on God's calendar and operating on His frequency. Beloved, *it is done, for when you declare boldly and confidently that it's completed and perfected,* the spirit of defacement flees.

Praises. Let me begin by saying that praise does not meet the battle—praise gathers the spoils. Praising God on credit is a guaranteed weapon against the spirit of defacement. Consider King Jehoshaphat, who defeated his enemies through praise while God fought the battle (2 Chronicles 20:20-22). Through praise, God took ownership of the battle, declaring, "The battle is mine." All the Israelites did—along with King Jehoshaphat—was cheer God on and continue praising Him.

† Praise breaks fortified walls.
† Praise drives the spirit of defacement away by declaring, *"Let God arise, and let His enemies be scattered"* (Psalm 68:1).
† Praise is supernatural immunity over God's blessings.

Why don't you pause now and praise God for the following and beyond:

† Praise God for that contract you bid for.
† Praise God for the healing you are trusting Him for.
† Praise God for debt relief and cancellation.
† Praise God for your future partner.
† Praise God for the deliverance of your children.
† Praise God for prosperity.
† Praise God for deliverance from addiction, depression, curses, bondage, stagnation, fear, deprivation, anger, sadness, and every burden laid before Him in prayer.

The Bible commands two things to be done continually and without ceasing: prayer and praise (1 Thessalonians 5:16-18). Why you may wonder: In prayer, we travail, but in praise we prevail. Furthermore, prayer takes you to God, but praise brings God to you, for *"He inhabits the praises of His people"* (Psalm 22:3).

Cheerful Giving. Giving is another way of defeating this spirit. It is a statement of gratitude, appreciation, and spiritual possession. Seed is powerful in possessing the gates of the enemy (Genesis 22:17). Gates are crucial, determining who occupies a city. Whoever controls the gate controls the activity within. Gateways are portals of intense spiritual warfare. A cheerful gift in response to your breakthrough secures the gates from encroachment or penetration. Give through alms. Give to your church to support kingdom work. Give to the man or woman of God who prays for you, as an expression of spiritual understanding and a strategy to retain the blessings you have received. Release your gift today in response to what God has already done—and your gates will be secured.

Speaking Over Your Blessings. Words are powerful tools to beautify everything God has given you. Speaking the Word of God over your life, business, and family grants heavenly immunity and drives away the spirit of defacement. I declare today over your life that the spirit of defacement is overthrown. Hallelujah! Rejoice over your blessings now, for there is no more sorrow, no more pain, no more regret or disappointment—in Jesus' name. Be joyful always. Sing a new song. *"When the Lord turned again the captivity of Zion, we were like them that dream"* (Psalm 126:1). You sowed in tears, but you shall reap in joy.

Say, "Thank You, Jesus."

The Battle Is Over

It is my greatest joy to declare to you today that the battle is over in your life (Exodus 14:13-14). The enemy has tried, in countless ways, to steal your blessings, delay your progress, and cloud your vision. But now, after walking together through his strategies, you are equipped with knowledge, discernment, and spiritual authority to stand firmly against every scheme of darkness (2 Corinthians 2:11). Victory belongs to those who understand the battlefield, for *"through knowledge shall the just be delivered"* (Proverbs 11:9).

I pray that this journey through the pages of this book has brought clarity to the struggles that have long weighed on your heart. Perhaps it has illuminated the puzzles, confusions, and unexplainable circumstances that once discouraged you, making life feel uncertain or unfair. My deepest hope is that this work will not remain merely a book on your shelf, but a spiritual heritage, a lamp shining in darkness, a glimmer of hope lighting the way through your tunnel of uncertainty.

The enemy may have stolen from you in the days of ignorance, but now it is time to reclaim everything that belongs to you (Joel 2:25). Rise in victorious confidence, knowing that Christ has already secured the triumph (1 Corinthians 15:57). Step boldly into the promises of God, for they are sure, and they are yours (2 Peter 1:3-4).

Do not live timidly. Do not apologize for walking in the fullness of life that God has ordained for you. **Stand tall, walk boldly, and embrace the abundant life that is your inheritance in Christ. Your purpose is divine. Your destiny is certain. And the God who called you is faithful to bring it to completion.

Now is the time to rise. To live. To fulfill your calling. Let this be the moment you step into victory—not as a distant hope, but as a present reality. The battle is over. The victory is yours. Rejoice, and let your life shine as a testament to the faithfulness of God.

7

THE SPIRIT OF DIVINE BLESSINGS

God's blessings are not fleeting moments of comfort, but legacies designed to defend His name, His character, and His integrity across the ages.

As we approach the twilight of this journey, it is my deepest desire to reward your patience and perseverance by presenting you with the nature of the blessings that heaven has graciously delivered into your hands at least with some stories that reflect our similar challenges, strange trail, and unexplainable distress of life, but through divine intervention, the stories of these men and women turned around for better, inspiring us with hope and building our confidence that our stories too shall end in remarkable victories in Jesus' name. Time and space may not permit detailed exposition, yet the few examples revealed here will be more than enough to unveil the heart of the Giver—the Father of lights, from whom every good and perfect gift descends (James 1:17).

As we examine the distinctive cases of these individuals who walked with God and trusted Him as their Source, it became more clearer that they were upheld by an **unseen hand**, guided by a **hidden Presence**, strengthened by a **divine Companion** who walked their roads, fought their battles, and whispered courage into their trembling hearts (Isaiah 41:10). They survived the furnace heated sevenfold, yet emerged without the smell of smoke (Daniel 3:27). They multiplied in the face of oppression, flourishing like Israel in Egypt where *"the more they were afflicted, the more they multiplied and grew"* (Exodus 1:12). They reaped a hundredfold harvest in a dry and foreign land, provoking the envy of nations (Genesis 26:12-14). Their wealth created fame, and their wisdom was sought by queens and nobles, as the nations traveled far to hear the counsel placed upon their lips (1 Kings 10:1-9). Dominion was given to them as they fought battles and subdued nations, their strength renewed like the eagle's (Psalm 103:5) and their courage kindled like fire in their bones. Not only were they blessed, but God swore by Himself that generations after them would inherit the blessing (Hebrews 6:13-14).

These men and women were immortalized by God, their stories preserved as sacred markers upon the path of time, signaling that His blessings are not fleeting moments of comfort, but legacies designed to defend His name, His character, and His integrity across the ages, for every blessing carries a pulse of eternity, every gift echoes the heart of the Giver, and every divine act writes another line in the story heaven is telling through us. By considering the examples below—what I will call divine blessings—our hearts gain fresh confidence that no matter where we stand today, no matter the sorrow that overwhelms or the burdens that press upon us, we have a God in heaven whose blessing not only delivers but also decorates.

Our part is simple: to call upon Him with confidence, knowing He hears. Our cry is not lost in some distant horizon; it rises like a gentle whisper into the ears of the Ever-Present Help in time of need (Psalm 46:1).This assurance becomes the anchor of our prayers. For *"this is the confidence we have in Him: that if we ask anything according to His will, He hears us. And if we know that He hears us, we know that we have the petitions we desired of Him"* (1 John 5:14-15). In this truth, faith finds its rest, hope finds its strength, and the soul discovers that **divine blessings are never out of reach, rather they descend upon those who dare to call, believe, and wait.**

Having seen the enemy's strategies—delay, detain, diversion, deception, and defacement of our blessings—it is now time to turn our focus toward the full benefits of salvation. In Christ, we are called to enjoy blessings without measure, to live lives of fulfillment, and to advance the initiatives of God's kingdom with power and purpose. We are not destined to leave faint footprints on the sands of time, footprints easily erased by the winds of life. No, our journey is meant to leave bold inscriptions upon the solid Rock, legacies that stand firm like the saints of old. These were not mere passersby through history; they carried mantles that shaped generations, leaving trails of faith for others to follow.

God is bringing you into such a season where your portion is doubled, where what was lost is restored, and where your influence multiplies beyond expectation. *"Instead of your shame you shall have double; and instead of confusion you shall rejoice in your portion"* (Isaiah 61:7). You are stepping into a chapter where **grace flows freely,** blessings abound, and purpose shines with new clarity. What God is pouring upon you is not merely for survival, but for impact so that you may thrive, build, bless, and leave a mantle for those who come after you. You are coming into your season of double portion. Walk boldly, for the Lord has gone before you.

Welcome to a new chapter, one not written by human hands, but inscribed by the pen of divine blessings. This is the dawn of a season where grace speaks louder than your past, where mercy outshines every former shadow, and where the fingerprints of God begin to decorate every line of your story. Step into this chapter with confidence, for the Author of your destiny writes with intention, precision, and love. His words do not fade; His promises do not fail; His blessings do not run dry.

This is not merely a continuation of life; It is an unveiling, a rising, a divine announcement that your life is shifting into alignment with God's purpose. Therefore, my esteemed reader, let hope breathe again, let expectation rise again, for the same God who began this good work in you will surely complete it (Philippians 1:6).

Divine Blessings and Their Nature

Divine blessings are far more than material abundance, answered prayers, or moments of supernatural intervention as we have seen from the very introduction of this book and other chapters. They are *expressions of God's nature*, flowing from His heart and carrying His intention for our lives. To understand divine blessings is to understand *How* God works, *Why* He gives, and *What* His blessings are designed to accomplish.

Below are deeper insights that reveal the true essence of divine blessings and why God is insisting that you are *Blessed by the Best*:

<u>*Divine blessings are through covenant, Abrahamic blessings*</u>. God does not bless randomly; He blesses *covenant-ally*. Every blessing in Scripture is connected to His promise, oath, or covenant. *"My covenant I will not break, nor alter the word that has gone out of My lips"* (Psalm 89:34). This means blessings are anchored in God's integrity, not human performance. Returning to this covenant through salvation is not merely a *personal decision*—it is a *positional reality*. What does this mean? When you chose to become a citizen of heaven through salvation, God took a covenant stance, placing you among those who partake of "the inheritance of the saints in light" (Colossians 1:12). Salvation is not only forgiveness; it is placement, identity, and access. It ushers you into a realm where divine promises become your portion, where grace becomes your garment, and where blessings flow not by merit but by covenant.

Scripture declares that God has *"blessed us with all spiritual blessings in heavenly places in Christ"* (Ephesians 1:3). These blessings are countless, immeasurable gifts wrapped in mercy, provision anchored in promise, and favor rooted in eternal love. To return to this covenant, therefore, is to step into what already belongs to you: a life aligned with divine purpose, a heart sustained by heavenly hope, and a destiny secured by the God who calls you His own. While salvation opens the door, covenant secures the inheritance. And you, redeemed, restored, repositioned, only walk boldly in the blessings that cannot be numbered by faith—*"the just shall live by faith"* (Romans 1:17).

*Divine blessings always align with **purpose***. God blesses purposefully. Every blessing carries intention, direction, and divine agenda. When anything ceases to fulfill the purpose for which it was created, *abuse becomes inevitable*. This truth echoes through Scripture: *"The LORD has made everything for its purpose"* (Proverbs 16:4). Blessings detached from purpose lose their brilliance; blessings embraced with understanding become instruments of destiny. All through the scriptures, God never blesses without purpose. His blessings are tools for assignment, not trophies for display. Adam was blessed to be fruitful and govern creation (Genesis 1:28). Abraham was blessed to be a blessing to nations (Genesis 12:2-3). "I will bless you" is God's promise; "You shall be a blessing" is your purpose. For the blessing is not merely received, but it is released. As God said to Abraham, *"I will bless you… and you shall be a blessing"* (Genesis 12:2). While His blessings fill your barns; His purpose directs your steps-for whenever God blesses, He empowers a person to fulfill His divine agenda.

Divine blessings transform character before circumstances. God's first work is always internal. Blessing begins in the heart before it shows up in the hands. Joseph's journey, from pit to prison to palace, shows God shaping character so the blessing could rest securely (Genesis 50:20). Many seek a quick remedy for life's pressing troubles. And rightly so, God is able. He turns water into wine (John 2:1-11), opens the eyes of the blind (John 9:1-7), and speaks worlds into being (Psalm 33:9). His power has never been in question. Yet the heart of divine blessing is not instant change, but inner transformation. For what God gives, only character shaped by His hand can sustain.

While many desire a sudden breakthrough, they resist the very process that forms the character capable of stewarding it—the renewal of the mind (Romans 12:2), the maturity of the soul (James 1:4), the strengthening of the inner man (Ephesians 3:16). God works from within, patiently chiseling His likeness upon man, as a potter shapes clay (Jeremiah 18:6). These divine pressures—renewal, discipline, pruning, testing—are not punishments; they are the tools of transformation, forging in us the nature that can comprehend the true purpose of God's blessing.

It is this transformed nature that aligns with the God who owns "the cattle on a thousand hills" (Psalm 50:10), "the silver and the gold" (Haggai 2:8), "the earth and all its fullness" (Psalm 24:1). He owns everything without altering His holiness, integrity, or unchanging nature (Malachi 3:6). This is His goal for man: not merely to receive blessing, but to become a vessel worthy of carrying it.

Consider Joseph. His character was proven in the furnace of betrayal. His spirit of forgiveness shone toward the brothers who sold him (Genesis 50:20). His loyalty and purity were evident in Pharaoh's palace, where even a pagan king declared, *"Can we find such a one as this, a man in whom is the Spirit of God?"* (Genesis 41:38). But many today abandon their faith for crumbs, trading eternal glory for temporal comfort. Once-humble hearts swell with pride at the scent of prosperity. Power unmixed with transformation becomes a beastly force.

Elisha looked into the soul of Hazael and wept, for he foresaw that the servant who spoke humbly would become cruel once he grasped the throne (2 Kings 8:11–13). So it is with any untransformed heart holding power or wealth—like a wild beast given a crown! God's blessings are never merely rewards; they are preparations. They are not designed to inflate us, but to refine us. To make us men and women whose nature mirrors His own, so that what He gives will not destroy us, but reveal His glory through us. True blessing purifies motives, deepens humility, and builds spiritual capacity.

We must walk in discernment with hearts bold enough to embrace the naked truth and to discern the difference between a spirit of delay and the Divine Sculptor shaping our souls for the blessings we cry out for. For what many believers mistakenly viewed as delay could be the Potter's hands pressing, turning, breaking, remaking and fashioning vessels worthy of glory (Jeremiah 18:6). Do not stall the purposes of God through unyielded will, wrestling shadows and calling it warfare, while the true battle is your surrender.

Divine blessings require surrender, not striving. Divine blessings flow where there is obedience, faith, and alignment with God's will. They are not earned; they are received through surrender. *"If you are willing and obedient, you shall eat the good of the land"* (Isaiah 1:19). Where striving ends is where surrender begins, for striving births only exhaustion; leaning on God births surrender, a holy dependence upon Him for every blessing. Unfortunately, many live out of balance, out of shape, and out of alignment because they continually try to bend God toward their own will, as though the Almighty could be compelled by human insistence. Some even attempt to force God's hand through what they call *radical prayer* or by misusing the phrase, *"the kingdom suffers violence"* (Matthew 11:12). My friend, pause and re-evaluate your request. God will only commit Himself to what He has commanded (Isaiah 55:11). Prayer is never meant to gratify our lusts or support petitions made "amiss" (James 4:3).

Consider Jacob. He wrestled with the Angel of the Lord through the night (Genesis 32:24-30).The Angel acknowledged that Jacob had strength to contend with God and with men. But could it be that Jacob was attempting to bend God toward his old nature, the nature hidden in the very name—Jacob, *a supplanter, deceiver, manipulator*? His identity crisis was laid bare. The Angel asked one piercing question: "What is your name?" Jacob answered quickly, "My name is Jacob," and there it was: Jacob the fighter, Jacob the schemer, Jacob the usurper, still striving for control, still trying to make God yield to him. But the Angel declared, "Your name shall be called Israel, "meaning *one who rules under God*. To become Israel, Jacob had to learn surrender. So God touched the socket of his thigh, and the strength he once relied on crumbled.

Jacob wrestled for a blessing—not material wealth, for he already possessed that—but for something deeper: a transformed identity, a covenant secured through obedience and surrender. Divine blessing demands sur-render so that God's covenant extends beyond the individual and His promises are fulfilled through a yielded vessel. So let me ask you: Are you still fighting from ego, selfishness, pride, or rebellion? Are you wrestling through disobedience while asking God to bless you?

Beloved, God does not bless a mess. Learn the sacred art of surrender, and you will understand the true cry of

Jacob: "I will not let You go unless You bless me." Not the cry of stubborn striving, but the cry of a heart finally yielded.

Divine blessings carry God's presence, not just His provision. The greatest blessing is God Himself; all other gifts flow like rivers from the fountain of His presence. The priestly benediction begins, *"The Lord bless you and keep you... and give you peace"* (Numbers 6:24-26). Notice that no material treasure is named, only God, for everything within His presence endures, and nothing without His presence is guaranteed. His presence is the light that interprets every provision. Without Him, blessings become burdens, riches become thorns, and abundance becomes a mirage.

If wealth alone secured joy, then the powerful and prosperous would be the happiest among men. Yet many who stand tall in the world lie crushed within, tormented by fear, depression, and despair. From the beginning, God placed man at the center of creation that all things might harmonize under His glory (Genesis 1:26-28). As David sang, *"The heavens declare the glory of God"* (Psalm 19:1). True blessing springs from the holy union between the Provider and His provision, for without Him, even Eden becomes wilderness. So here is the mathematical equation worthy of consideration: $P(p)=dp$, where P stands for person, small p stands for presence, and dp is equal to divine provision.

When David fell into sin, his deepest cry was not for his throne or crown, but for God's presence: *"Cast me not away from Your presence"* (Psalm 51:11). He understood that fullness of joy is found only before God's face, and eternal pleasure at His right hand (Psalm 16:11). My friend, this is the hidden fountain of a joyful life—the peace that surpasses understanding, the strength that renews youth like the eagle (Philippians 4:7; Psalm 103:5).

Saul sat on a throne yet lived in torment; he needed David's harp to quiet his troubled soul (1 Samuel 16:23). Solomon possessed gold without measure, yet concluded, *"Vanity of vanities"* (Ecclesiastes 1:2). This is the tragedy of blessings detached from their Source—provision without Presence, abundance without life. But God, rich in mercy, has given us His most precious gift—His voice that announces His presence. A voice that stills storms (Mark 4:39), strengthens the weary (Isaiah 40:29), steadies the trembling heart, and whispers courage into the dark night. His presence is the soul's true inheritance; His voice, the compass that guides us home. Where God's presence rests, peace, favor, and protection follow.

<u>*Divine blessings are often concealed in ordinary process.*</u> Blessings do not always appear as miracles; sometimes, they arrive disguised in unfamiliar forms. God's blessings often look unlike what we expect. Many times, they are misinterpreted, underestimated, or even ridiculed. Yet great things often come in small packages, and many glorious endings begin with painful beginnings.

Years ago, I preached a message titled "A Tree Within a Seed." Consider the rugged rod in Moses' hand—ordinary wood turned into a divine instrument of deliverance (Exodus 4:2-4). Think of the small lunch in the hands of a little boy, multiplied to feed thousands (John 6:9-11). Think of an inexperienced teenager, David, facing a seasoned warrior like Goliath (1 Samuel 17). A widow with nothing but a little oil used to cancel an overwhelming debt (2 Kings 4:1-7). God's anointed king found not in Jesse's proud eldest son but in forgotten David tending sheep (1 Samuel 16:11-13). Even a nameless little maid in Naaman's household held the key to his cleansing (2 Kings 5:2-3). This is the God whose ways are not our ways and whose thoughts soar far above ours (Isaiah 55:8-9). No wonder Scripture warns us, *"Do not despise the day of small things"* (Zechariah 4:10).

And mockery? Oh no—you are not alone. Goliath mocked David. Nathanael mocked Nazareth, asking, *"Can anything good come out of Nazareth?"* (John 1:46). When Saul prophesied with the prophets, people mocked saying, *"Is Saul also among the prophets?"* (1 Samuel 10:11-12). People have mocked your small beginnings. They have ridiculed your slow progress, your endurance, and your resilience. Some have profiled you because of your background or the color of your skin. But remember—there is always a Jabez who rises above pain, breaks generational patterns, and overturns every verdict of mockery (1 Chronicles 4:9-10).

This is how divine blessings often come—a strange process, a seed buried in the ground, a small opportunity, painful pruning, an unexpected relationship, or a shift that feels uncomfortable. It may be a season of loneliness that summons ravens to feed you (1 Kings 17:4-6), or a dried-up brook that redirects you to Zarephath for provision (1 Kings 17:7-9). It may even be blindness allowed so that the works of God might be displayed (John 9:1-3). Ordinary and unusual processes often conceal extraordinary blessings.

Our greatest liability in these moments is our obsession with where we came from, while neglecting where God is taking us. David admonishes, *"Fret not yourself"* (Psalm 37:1), for hidden within your temporary trial is a blessing preparing to reveal *"a far more exceeding and eternal weight of glory"* (2 Corinthians 4:17). A weight of glory incomparable to the burden you now endure—hallelujah! Hold fast your confession of faith, for your blessing is coming from the Best.

<u>*Divine blessings inspire diligence and responsibility*</u>. Every blessing carries a weight of stewardship. Adam was blessed, then instructed to tend and keep the garden (Genesis 2:15). The servants given talents were blessed to multiply, not bury (Matthew 25:14-30). God finished creation before He ever began it (Isaiah 46:10), yet He stepped into time to bring His finished work into manifestation. This is the mystery of His ways—He completes the masterpiece, then invites us to join Him in the unfolding. We are offered the tail end of the divine project, not to create it, but to participate in its becoming. Here is where diligence lifts a man before kings (Proverbs 22:29). Blessing never excuses responsibility. God gives seed so that we might have a harvest. He grows trees in the forest so we may craft furniture and shape beauty from them. When He instructed Moses to build the tabernacle *"according to the pattern shown on the mountain"* (Exodus 25:40), He anointed Bezalel and Oholiab with skill—artistry, embroidery, craftsmanship. The anointing was not for noise or spiritual display, but for diligent work. Think about it: anointed to be a good wife/husband, anointed to clean very well, anointed to drive safely, build

wisely, supervise responsibly, collaborate faithfully, and prosper along the way. You are the "anointed."

Many confuse spirituality with responsibility, but God blesses only the labor of the diligent. Even with all His power, He will allow the prey of the hunter to rot if the hunter refuses to roast it (Proverbs 12:27). Prayer is essential, but prayer without work is presumptive and irresponsible. Use whatever God has placed in your hands, and blessings will begin to flow. Hours spent in church and days spent in fasting are powerful only when translated into action—into labor, strategy, obedience, and steps toward the very petitions we pray for. Without this, the desert remains dry and the mountain unmoved. God moves when we move. He blesses effort, rewards diligence, and anoints productivity. Ghana leads the world in cocoa yet still imports chocolate. Nigeria raises cattle, its nomads roaming from north to east, yet it imports milk from the Netherlands. These nations pray with fire, yet their citizens journey to lands that turn raw materials into finished treasures.

Isaac sowed in the land and reaped a hundredfold (Genesis 26:12). Joseph applied wisdom, offering economic policy that lifted Egypt above nations (Genesis 41:33-57). Even today, the nations that pray the most are not necessarily the most productive. Why? Because prayer opens revelation, but revelation demands execution. The fastest-growing economies are constantly crafting new policies. World powers rise through innovation, invention, diligence, and skill. There is a time to pray and a time to work (Ecclesiastes 3:1). Divine blessings rest on what the hands are doing—work that is visible, not imagined, while arms remain folded. God blesses those who value what He gives and multiply it.

Divine blessings are generational. Divine blessings are powerful, cascading from one generation to another, flowing like a sacred river through the bloodline. *"The house of the righteous shall be blessed,"* Scripture declares, while *"the wealth of the wicked is an abomination"* (Proverbs 3:33; 21:27). Life is a marathon, not a sprint; therefore, the blessing of God does not carve mere monuments; it births movements.

Consider Abraham. God not only blessed him but made him an extension of blessing. Through Abraham, *"your seed shall be blessed"* and *"the blessing of Abraham"* would flow even to the Gentiles (Galatians 3:14). God called Abraham and Sarah the very **rock** from which we were hewn (Isaiah 51:1-2). Such is the nature of divine blessing; it outlives its vessel.

David, before he closed his eyes in death, handed Solomon a throne secured by covenant. Solomon testified to Hiram, *"The Lord my God has given me rest on every side; there is neither adversary nor evil occurrence"* (1 Kings 5:4). This is the fragrance of blessing: rest, security, and continuity. For the righteous, blessing becomes inheritance, children and children's children carrying the lamp forward (Proverbs 13:22). Yet Scripture also records families whose disobedience closed their lineage: the house of Eli stripped of priesthood (1 Samuel 2:30-36) and Ahab's dynasty cut off because of rebellion (1 Kings 21:21). While the wicked are extinguished; the righteous are preserved. And for the righteous, blessings do not die with the blessed—they travel, they descend, they endure. They shape stories for centuries, rewriting the history of families yet unborn. And so shall it be for you. Your children will inherit your honor, your lineage will preserve your dignity, and your descendants will carry your lamp in Jesus' name.

Divine blessings conquer opposing forces. We are not exempt from the schemes of the wicked, yet we are guaranteed victory in every battle. *"Many are the afflictions of the righteous, but the Lord delivers him out of them all"* (Psalm 34:19). To walk through *"the valley of the shadow of death"* unharmed and to pass through fire without the smell of smoke (Psalm 23:4; Daniel 3:27) is proof of a divine force at work in us.

From the beginning, the Creator knew the luciferous agenda, how the adversary would relentlessly pursue those who trust in the Lord. Yet every weapon he forms is neutralized (Isaiah 54:17), and divine blessing turns all things to work for the good of those who love God (Romans 8:28). Sorrow may linger through the night, but joy always rises at dawn (Psalm 30:5).

Do not expect the enemy to watch silently while you flourish in the courts of the Lord. He is rightly called "the adversary" (1 Peter 5:8). Yet God's blessing always prevails: Abraham suffered delay, yet God made his descendants uncountable (Genesis 15:5). Joseph endured betrayal and imprisonment, yet he rose as prime minister in Egypt (Genesis 41:41-43). Daniel faced the lion's den but emerged untouched, exalted above his haters (Daniel 6:16-23). Mordecai and Israel confronted extermination, yet God overturned Haman's conspiracy and honored His people (Esther 7:9-10). Jesus Christ met every temptation—and defeated even death itself (Hebrews 4:15; 1 Corinthians 15:55-57).

The end of a matter is always better than its beginning (Ecclesiastes 7:8). Divine blessing carves a path where none exists, granting a glorious conclusion to those who endure their trials. Peter and his brothers saw a dawn unlike the night they had toiled in vain; at Christ's word, their nets overflowed (Luke 5:1–7). So trust the blessing upon your life. Believe that all things will turn for the best. God is working—even when heaven seems silent, the road feels lonely, and the night stretches long.

Do not be deceived by the enemy's whisper, nor intimidated by the shadows of doubt. What God has spoken must come to pass. *"No weapon formed against you shall prosper, and every tongue that rises against you in judgment you shall condemn"* (Isaiah 54:17). Open your hands and your heart, for your blessings are ready to be received. They have been released by the One who turns seed into harvest and tears into joy (2 Corinthians 9:10). Do not shrink back in fear or hesitation, for His timing is flawless. Rejoice, beloved! Your blessings are not merely approaching; **they are here**. Embrace them. Celebrate them. Walk boldly in the overflowing abundance of God's unstoppable love, for you are truly Blessed by the Best!

CONGRATULATIONS!!!

About the Author

INNOCENT CHINEDU ODINIGWE

Apostle Innocent Chinedu Odinigwe is an apostle, preacher, teacher, and prophet devoted to unveiling God's will and guiding believers into lives marked by divine blessing, healing, purpose, and true freedom. His ministerial journey began in 1989, when he answered the call to salvation. A seasoned revivalist and former general leader of the Charismatic Renewal Movement in Nigeria, he has brought healing to many through fervent prayer, city-to-city revivals, and family deliverance. He has also confronted demonic powers and led many into liberty in Christ. As senior pastor of Miracle

Christian Center, a parish of the Redeemed Christian Church of God (RCCG), he ministers with a prophetic voice anchored in prayer, Scripture, and revelation—evidenced by countless testimonies of healing and deliverance flowing from the mantle and mandate upon his life.

His ministry reaches far beyond the pulpit. Through tangible compassion, he feeds and supports hundreds of widows and orphans, embodying a faith that works by love. A sought-after conference speaker and retreat facilitator, he is known for uniting spiritual depth with practical leadership. A devoted prayer warrior, he labors at the altar to confront evil vices, shift spiritual atmospheres, and enforce God's dominion on earth. He also serves as a board member of Prayer Academy, an institute dedicated to raising intercessors and prayer warriors for this generation.

Apostle Odinigwe holds a bachelor's degree in administration, a master's degree in clinical psychology, and an honorary Doctor of Divinity. He has been happily married to his wife, Josephine, for over twenty-seven years, and they are blessed with three children, Miriam, David, and Benjamin, and innumerable spiritual sons and daughters.

www.ingramcontent.com/pod-product-compliance
Lightning Source LLC
Chambersburg PA
CBHW072200160426
43197CB00012B/2464